GETTING OUT

GETTING OUT

HISTORICAL PERSPECTIVES ON LEAVING IRAQ

Edited by

Michael Walzer and Nicolaus Mills

A Dissent Book

PENN

University of Pennsylvania Press

Philadelphia

Published by
University of Pennsylvania Press
Philadelphia, Pennsylvania 19104-4112

Printed in the United States of America on acid-free paper
10   9   8   7   6   5   4   3   2   1

Library of Congress Cataloging-in-Publication Data

Getting out : historical perspectives on leaving Iraq / edited by Michael
Walzer and Nicolaus Mills.
p. cm.
ISBN: 978-0-8122-4216-4 (alk. paper)
Includes index.
1. Disengagement (Military science)—Case studies. 2. Imperialism—
Case studies. 3. Military history. 4. Iraq War, 2003–
5. Disengagement (Military science) 6. United States—Armed Forces—Iraq.
I. Walzer, Michael. II. Mills, Nicolaus.
U167.G48   2009
355.4—dc22   2009018801

To Eric Reeves,
who demonstrates every day
what one person can do for human rights.

Contents

GETTING IN/GETTING OUT

Introduction

Michael Walzer

EVENTUALLY everyone gets out—all the conquerors, all the imperial powers, all the occupying armies, even all the peacekeepers. Sooner or later, they leave. But "sooner or later" can be a hotly contested political question. Some imperial powers don't leave voluntarily; they are defeated and replaced by new imperialists—so the Byzantines were replaced by the Ottomans in the Balkans, the Germans by the British in East Africa, the Dutch by the Japanese (though only briefly) in Indonesia. Other imperial powers are defeated and overthrown, like the Nazis in the Second World War. What distinguishes these forced departures is that they don't involve a political decision. Peacekeeping, by contrast, always ends with a political decision, and so do most occupations. It is the premeditated and much debated decision to withdraw that we are interested in here.

Why did the imperial or occupying power decide to leave? How did its political and military leaders manage the withdrawal? Did they take with them people who might be at risk if left behind? What were the immediate consequences of their departure? These are the questions we asked our contributors to address with regard to seven historical cases: Britain's departure from the American colonies and from India, the French withdrawal from Algeria, Israel's unilateral withdrawal from Gaza, and the United States decision to leave (or not) the Philippines, Korea, and Vietnam. There are other famous withdrawals we could have considered: the British from Palestine, the French from Vietnam, the Portuguese from Angola, the Russians from East Germany. And there are withdrawals sure to come, somewhere down the road—NATO from Kosovo, for example. But our seven cases, we believe, raise the critical issues Americans need to think about today with regard to Iraq.

Iraq is our primary interest, but we want to see it in comparative perspective and to learn, if that is possible, from what might be called the experience of exit—the history of political and military retreats. Many books and articles have been written about leaving this country or that one, but the larger issue, leaving itself, hasn't been addressed with the seriousness it requires.

This is the right time in American political history to address the exit experience—and to worry specifically about the difficulties certain to arise as we leave Iraq. So we asked three writers who have been engaged with the Iraq story from its beginning to read the historical essays and then to write about the (sooner or later) U.S. withdrawal. Nicolaus Mills's account of "getting in" to Iraq is intended to set the stage for the arguments about getting out.

We also need to worry about a more general, and critically important, question: What are the moral and political principles that should govern the withdrawal of imperial and occupying armies? Put aside for now all the prior questions: How did they get in? Was their military entrance just or unjust? What was the character of their stay? Those are important questions, and they will determine our view of the decision to withdraw. We will think withdrawal urgent and necessary if we view the conquest or occupation in negative terms—and that is usually the right way to view it. But it isn't always the right way, as Fred Smoler's piece on South Korea suggests: here is a case where a just war led to a long-term and ultimately highly successful military presence, its character more like peacekeeping (deterring the North) than occupation. And when withdrawal is morally necessary, as in many of the imperial cases, it isn't necessarily prudent or right to withdraw immediately. The backward-looking and historical judgments are only sometimes the crucial ones. We also need to look forward: even a morally imperative withdrawal, like that of the British from India, might rightly be postponed in the face of a looming disaster. Rajeev Bhargava argues that a British decision to stay on, if only for another year, might have avoided the mass killing that followed on their hasty 1947 departure. Withdrawals are good and bad, just and unjust, even when we consider them without reference to their prehistory.

Every withdrawal is managed, first of all, in the interests of the soldiers and citizens of the imperial or occupying power. Their safety is always a critical consideration—though the presence of a *colon* or settler population that doesn't want to leave (as in Algeria and Gaza) makes things very difficult for the withdrawing army. It has to assist, sometimes to force, its own citizens to leave, often in circumstances that put them, and the soldiers doing the assisting or forcing, at risk. And then the government of the home country has to organize the resettlement of the settlers. But there is another, larger, responsibility—to the people of the conquered or occupied country. It is their society and their lives that have been disrupted by foreigners claiming to rule over them (always for their own good), and when the foreigners depart they must make sure that their departure isn't a further, disastrous disruption.

Simply by being there, they have acquired obligations—and this without regard to whether we think they should or shouldn't have been there. It is a commonplace of moral life that people doing the right thing are often required to do more and more right things. So foreigners intervening to stop a massacre or interrupt a campaign of ethnic cleansing find themselves responsible for the well-being of the people they have rescued and then for the political and economic reconstruction of the country they have invaded. But foreigners can also take on responsibilities by doing bad things—like trying to conquer or colonize another country, or establish a satellite regime, or extend a sphere of influence. When the project fails, the foreign soldiers and officials must work as best they can to leave behind a country at peace and a new regime capable of keeping the peace.

The new regime won't necessarily be liberal or democratic. It may be formed, for example, by a movement for national liberation that is highly centralized in its organization and violent in its politics, and the centralization and violence won't disappear at the moment of independence. But this can't be an excuse for staying—not, at least, if the movement has won what we called in Vietnam "the battle for hearts and minds." Earlier on, perhaps, the imperial or occupying power might have acted to create a better successor, but once it has failed it has to leave. The French negotiated their Algerian exit with a group, the Front de Libération Nationale (FLN), that they must have known would establish an authoritarian regime. Nonetheless, negotiating was the right thing to do, given the moral and political failure of French rule. The FLN represented Algerian self-determination even though its future course was not going to be determined by the people of Algeria.

With regard to a democratic succession, always preferable if it is possible, the British didn't fail in America or in India. Nor did the Americans fail in the Philippines or Korea (though the victory of democracy in the latter countries took a long time, and the road was hard). Of course, when the imperial or occupying power sets up, and then props up, a new regime, the legitimacy of that regime will always be in question—it will be called, and it may well be, the puppet of its creators. But given enough political space in which to operate, it can sometimes acquire the support of its own people and the capabilities that go with sovereignty, and then it can negotiate the departure of its patrons and even insist on tough and binding terms. Many Americans, both those who opposed and those who supported the war in Iraq, hope for that sort of an ending—a withdrawal on terms set by the government or, in Brendan O'Leary's vision, the federated governments, that we leave behind.

One of the hardest tests that the withdrawing forces face has to do with their loyalty, or lack of it, to the men and women who supported the empire or the occupation or who, whatever their politics, worked for the foreigners. Hasty exits, with many vulnerable people left behind, are common enough in the history of empires and military occupations, but they are, and should be, a source of shame. The people left behind are rarely left in peace. They are harassed, persecuted, killed, or sent to camps; or they hide and flee, like the Vietnamese "boat people," desperate to escape from communist rule. Our memories of the Second World War have given "collaborators" a bad name—which is often deserved. Many of the people who come forward to help the imperial or occupying forces are opportunists or sycophants, servants of the powerful, whoever the powerful are. But not all of them are like that, and in any case it doesn't matter. Once the time for withdrawal comes, they and their families are at risk, and they have to be helped. The withdrawing forces have clear obligations, not, of course, to criminals, not to murderers or thieves among the collaborators, but to all the "ordinary" men and women who worked with them.

It is worth pondering the fact that the British in the 1780s took thousands of Loyalist families out of the new American republic, where they would certainly have had a hard time, while the French in Algeria and the Americans in Vietnam failed to honor commitments to their own loyalists. Except for the richest among them, the British Loyalists were taken not to cosmopolitan Britain but only to colonial Canada. Still, given the size of eighteenth-century ships, this was a major undertaking. I don't think that it has been matched since. The American invasion of Iraq and the subsequent civil war have sent millions of refugees fleeing to Syria and Jordan, and we have done nothing to help them. And, so far, very few of the people who worked with us in Iraq and who are at risk as a result have been brought to the United States—or actively helped to go anywhere else. George Packer stresses the critical importance of this moral failure and suggests how it might be remedied.

Withdrawal is also shaped by domestic politics in the withdrawing country, where it is common for right-wing forces to oppose the exit or to insist that it should take place only "later," while the left is in favor of "sooner," if not *right now*. The two positions were first established in parliamentary debates about Britain's American colonies, and they have been pretty standard ever since. There are exceptions, of course. Some Republican right-wingers opposed the U.S. intervention in Korea and would have been glad to see us leave as soon as possible, and the left and right positions may well be blurred or even reversed in cases of humanitarian intervention and extended peacekeeping operations. But most often imperial adventures and military occupations are viewed with enthusiasm on the right and with skepticism or hostility on the left. In the cases of Algeria, Vietnam, and Gaza (Palestine), this disagreement took on a fairly ferocious character. The political divisions in the withdrawing states went very deep, with long-lasting effects. These divisions may have made for withdrawals that were not as well planned, the consequences not as carefully considered, as they might have been.

Disagreements over Iraq in the United States in 2009 do not seem as divisive or as dangerous as in these other cases—though our three writers certainly represent significantly different and opposing positions. I am not sure why the disagreements are less dangerous to American political stability than similar disagreements have been in other countries. Perhaps the manifest incompetence of our Iraq policy, after the first three weeks of the war, has produced a widespread disgust with the occupation, not only on the left, which should make withdrawal easier to manage, at least at home. But what kind of internal debates and divisions will there be if things go very badly after we leave?

We might also ask what happens farther down the road. Britain and the United States have a "special relationship," though it took another war and many decades before that relationship was worked out. Britain and India have friendly diplomatic relations and strong cultural ties. The French have important commercial interests in postcolonial Algeria—and cultural ties too, though these are probably less openly acknowledged than in the case of Britain and India. Gaza and Israel are still at gunpoint, and the Israeli withdrawal doesn't seem to have brought peace with the Palestinians any closer. The Republic of the Philippines is an American political and military ally. We still have large numbers of troops in South Korea, though the government there is increasingly independent, able to oppose U.S. policy and stick to its guns—a tribute, I think, to the character of our long military presence. The United States has made a kind of peace with Vietnam, though any close relationship looks far away. It would be nice to find a correlation between just and justly managed withdrawals, on the one hand, and future good relations, on the other, but I don't think that there is one. Iraq after the U.S. withdrawal will certainly not be a "friend" of the sort that the Bush administration hoped for. Whether it will be a friend at all over the coming decades, or, more important, whether its government will be committed to democracy at home or abroad, or to international law, or to peace with its neighbors—all this remains to be seen.

But the principles that guide justice in withdrawing are local in time and space; we don't have to speculate on the decades to come. Years ago, philosopher John Rawls argued that distributive justice requires close attention to the position of the least well-off people. By analogy, justice in withdrawing requires close attention to the safety of the most vulnerable people. The possible victims of ethnic or religious violence, or of civil war, or of retribution and revenge at the hands of the successor regime—these people must be looked after. For Brendan O'Leary, the most vulnerable people in Iraq are the Kurds, and he writes with particular attention to their safety. Protecting the vulnerable is a centrally important obligation of the withdrawing army, even as it also, legitimately, aims to protect its own soldiers. The character and extent of the risks faced by groups like the Kurds are sure to be politically contested—minimized by those in favor of withdrawing "sooner," exaggerated by those in favor of "later." I doubt that strict objectivity can be a moral obligation, but a serious effort to produce the best possible estimate of the dangers ahead is morally obligatory.

Meeting those dangers may take longer than the advocates of "sooner" acknowledge—this is George Packer's argument with regard to Iraq. Prudential judgments are needed in each case. But we know from the long history of imperialism and military occupation that somewhere down the road withdrawal will be necessary, and it will happen. Even just occupations must end. Even long-term peacekeeping operations will draw down at some point, when the people whose peace is being "kept" decide that they no longer need the keeping. At some point the imperial or occupying armies must face the political and moral imperative best expressed by the old English word: "Begone!" They must try to ensure stability in the aftermath of their departure. They must do what they can, even when they don't have the moral or political authority to do very much, to create a successor regime that fits the model of "self-determination." They must protect the people who most need protection. And they must go.

LESSONS FROM
THE PAST

1

No Exit but Victory:
Britain and the American Colonies

STANLEY WEINTRAUB

How does one recognize the looming inevitable? In the 1760s, the British, having defeated the French in America and expanded George III's overseas empire, saw only profit and prestige ahead. A New England cleric, the Reverend Samuel Cooper, told his congregation that the colonists were indebted "not only for their present Security and Happiness, but, perhaps for their very Being, to the paternal Care of the Monarch." The legitimacy of royal rule was little questioned. In that future seedbed of sedition, Boston, Thomas Foxcroft declared, "Above all, we owe our humble *Thanks* to his Majesty and with loyal Hearts full of joyous Gratitude, we bless the *King*, for his Paternal Goodness in sending such effectual Aids to his American Subjects. . . when we needed the Royal Protection."

A seven-year war 3,000 miles from home, when travel time was measured in months, had pinched the British economy. Why not, then, have the colonists, who had been rescued from the wicked French, pay something for their own protection? It was a petty stamp tax on printed paper, a bargain fee (a quarter of what Britons at home paid) on imported tea. It would go to quartering Redcoats to keep away marauding Indians, or to inhibit revengeful "Frogs."

This imperial logic escaped its beneficiaries. Outspoken colonists resented paying anything on their own behalf, claiming lack of representation in Parliament, the tax-raising body in remote London. But that complaint was only the tip of the trade iceberg. Colonists by law could not manufacture weapons or ammunition (or much else) for their own defense. British industry at home was sustained by commercial barriers. Americans were to supply the raw materials for making the goods they would have to buy as finished products.

Within a decade, objections about taxes, trade, and troops had plucked the gilded genie from the transatlantic bottle. Colonial farmers, craftsmen, and merchants began proposing a new concept, *liberty*, as a solution to their discontent. In Britain, complacent merchants, manufacturers, and landowners saw only ignorance, ingratitude, and greed motivating the radicalized handful of New England Yankees, who—despite a way with words—lacked arms and fighting zeal. In the seemingly tractable South, Tory planters—self-styled aristocrats—prospered alongside a noisy rabble and illiterate backwoodsmen. Samuel Johnson grumbled that deprivation of the "rights of Englishmen" was an unrealistic grievance. Americans were no less represented in Parliament than most inhabitants on his own side of the water, who lived in increasingly teeming districts excluded from seats in Parliament. Americans were "a race of convicts, and ought to be thankful for any thing we allow them short of hanging."

Did the Establishment foresee unwelcome change? Could it maintain the imperial equilibrium by granting token seats—unlikely ever to be occupied—in the House of Commons, as London was an ocean away and members unsalaried, or by prudently tucking Redcoats away in obscure barracks; or by relaxing commercial restrictions,

more professional than the poorly equipped, ragged, undisciplined patchwork amateurs serving short enlistments and unlikely to stay on for further service. The *London Morning Post* published a list of rebel generals ostensibly ridiculed for their prewar occupations—a boat builder, a bookseller, a servant, a milkman, a jockey, a clerk. It was a covert satire on British snobbery, implying that commanders of noble birth were overmatched by officers reaching the top by merit in classless America. Misguided generalship was compounded by civilian arrogance at Whitehall. Winston Churchill would write: "Rarely has British strategy fallen into such a multitude of errors. Every principle of war was either violated or disregarded."

Although the British had a surplus of brass, as the war dragged on it became frustrating to fill the ranks. When it became difficult to raise more Redcoats, Parliament obstinately authorized hiring thousands of mercenaries from German statelets ("Hessians," although not all were from Hesse) and constructing warships by the dozen. The amphibious assault on Long Island and Manhattan employed an armada not surpassed in numbers until D-Day in 1944, yet in remote upstate New York in 1777 Burgoyne and his army, bereft of reinforcements, surrendered at Saratoga.

General William Howe took the rebel capital, Philadelphia, chasing George Washington into woeful winter quarters at Valley Forge. Still, Washington was winning merely by keeping his army alive while imperial overstretch took its toll. The insurgency thrived on British attrition. With more land to occupy and control than he had troops to accomplish the job, Howe scuttled back to New York the next spring, explaining later from London, once he had been replaced (and promoted), that professional soldiers lost to shot and disease would be difficult to replace from across an ocean, while the upstart Americans could recruit marginally trained militiamen close at hand. He would "never expose the troops . . . where the object is inadequate."

The War at Home

If the object was not worth the effort, why not abandon it? Undeterred, other generals succeeded Howe. Never numerous, local loyalist volunteers were decreasing, while further foreign hirelings were largely unaffordable under dwindling budgets, captive now to the contagion of pessimism and new parliamentary parsimony. Even the country landowners, the conservative backbone of the regime, were becoming disillusioned, as a wry "Dialogue between a Country Squire and his Tenant" suggested in the *London Gazeteer* in 1778:

> *Tenant*: Pray, Squire, when do you think the war will end?
> *Squire*: At Doomsday, *perhaps* sooner; but this is certain, the nation is almost ruined, and we country gentlemen are the greatest sufferers.

As an unbridled press revealed, returning casualties and the declining standards for enlistment made soldiering a grim option, largely for the jobless and the poor. "An Exact Representation of Manchester Recruits," captioning a cartoon of weird, dehumanized volunteers, illustrated the increasing national pain. "The Master of the Arses, or the Westminster Volunteers" showed six motley recruits spurred on, front and rear, by bayonet-bearing Redcoats, one inductee stumbling with a crutch and stick, another on gouty, swathed legs. "The Church Militant" satirized an equally useless dimension of belligerence. In that broadside, a group of clergy, some lean and ascetic, others stout and gross, all led by obtuse bishops, sing "O Lord Our God, Arise and Scatter Our Enemies." Desperation about the war was out in the open.

Decades later, Charles Dickens in *Barnaby Rudge* imagined a scene in the aptly named Black Lion tavern in the late 1770s, in which the barkeep observes scornfully as a recruiting sergeant offers his spiel,

"I'm told there ain't a deal of difference between a fine man and another one, when they're shot through and through."

The sergeant suggests to potential enlistees a life of wine, women, and glory, and a timid voice pipes, "Supposing you should be killed, sir?" Confidently, the Redcoat responds, "What then? Your country loves you, sir; his Majesty King George the Third loves you; your memory is honoured, revered, respected; . . . your name's wrote down at full length in a book in the War Office. Damme, gentlemen, we must all die some time or other, eh!" Pages later, the publican's son, who fell for the sales pitch and has returned from Savannah, sits quietly in the tavern with one sleeve empty. "It's been took off," his father explains, "at the defence of the Salwanners. . . . In America, where the war is." To his listeners, it is all meaningless.

While losses, prices, and taxes fueled anxiety, no effective tactics surfaced to put down the rebellion. End-the-war adherents were an increasing yet still powerless minority. Since the "experiment" of putting the Americans down was failing, the *St. James's Chronicle* editorialized, Britain should "withdraw in time with a good grace, and declare them INDEPENDENT." Although the House of Lords remained firmly behind the king, in the Commons a former general and Cabinet minister, Henry Seymour Conway, moved that "this mad war" should "no longer be pursued." The motion failed by one vote. "We are not only *patriots out of place*," Sir George Savile, a Yorkshire MP, remarked gloomily to the marquis of Rockingham, "but patriots *out of the opinion of the public.*" Rockingham advised waiting "till the Publick are actually convinced of the calamitous State we are in." That would come only after the futile campaigns of Charles Cornwallis in the presumably safe American South. Not many months after, Rockingham would be the first peace prime minister.

Cornwallis busied himself evading defeat, but he ran out of alternatives late in 1781, once the French intervened by land and sea. Third forces are often crucial. Uninterested in American ideals about liberty and equality, the French were determined to give the British a black eye and arrived in Yorktown before a rescue fleet from New York. Abroad, few had been listening to radicals like Josiah Tucker, an Anglican divine and amateur economist, who in a pamphlet, *Cui Bono*, called for getting out. America, he charged, had become a "millstone" round the neck of Britain. "If we ourselves have not the wisdom to cut the Rope, and let the Burthen fall off, the Americans have kindly done it for us."

As Cornwallis surrendered at Yorktown, a British band played "The World turn'd Upside Down." After further weeks of national dismay, George Germain, pushed to resign, was rewarded for his sacrifice with a viscountcy. A broadside cartoon, "Three Thousand Leagues beyond the Cannon's Reach," portrayed him satirically yet realistically as unable to direct military affairs from distant London. His office as secretary for America was soon abolished by Rockingham's reform government.

The Long Withdrawal

The British had no exit strategy other than victory. Capitulation and a draft treaty negotiated in Paris the next year with the grudgingly recognized United States required evacuating troops from the few Atlantic seaports they still held and keeping faith somehow with loyalists still within British boundaries. There were also thousands of prisoners of war to be paroled, held hostage in vain by Congress for payment of their upkeep. The hard and possibly thankless decisions were left to the pragmatic last Redcoat commander, Sir Guy Carleton, who, with a mere knighthood, eyed a peerage for his services. (He would get it.) Fleets of transports would evacuate Charleston, Wilmington in North Carolina, and tightly held Savannah, taking with them prominent but angry loyalists who had to abandon their properties. Most were promised only a sailing to Halifax and resettlement in the sparsely populated Maritime Provinces. Diehards were granted six hundred very likely untillable acres; officers choosing Canada were offered fifteen hundred acres; and men in the ranks could look forward to a meager fifty. Some troops opting for further duty were sent to the West Indies to garrison sugar islands against the French.

Under occupation beyond New York and Long Island were isolated frontier posts on the Canadian border held for payment of colonial debts acknowledged in the treaty. As the financial settlements were made unwillingly and late, Forts Niagara, Oswego, Presque Isle, Mackinaw, and Detroit would not be relinquished until the mid-1790s. The Treaty of Paris called for the British departure to be accomplished "with all convenient speed," but the major remaining enclave of New York was held by Carleton until he had confirmation of acceptable guarantees for withdrawal of his troops and local loyalists. About 3,000 slaves within British lines were permitted to leave with owners who certified them. Others were reclaimed by Washington's "commissioners" (for lack of documentation) as "American property," while most aged, sick, and otherwise helpless slaves were cynically abandoned to freedom as worthless for labor. Ironically, the chattels left behind were liberated for less than idealistic reasons, but Washington, after all, was a slaveholder.

For Carleton, getting out was a logistic nightmare. It had taken 479 vessels to bring the first 39,000 troops to New York in July 1776. Reembarking the occupiers and their equipage required much more—several months and hundreds of sailings and return sailings through early December 1783, as frantic sympathizers by the thousands (29,244 evacuees from New York to gloomy Nova Scotia alone), along with their most prized goods, were assured accommodation. Few—only the wealthy elite and those closely associated with the royal government—were eligible for immigration to England, where Benedict Arnold had already arrived, to no acclaim, with his family.

The British had no interest in housing, employing, or feeding their miserable and burdensome transatlantic cousins.

Humiliated, George III threatened to abdicate in favor of the playboy Prince of Wales, but prudently dropped the idea. Rather, in a rare attack of realism, the king belatedly recognized the first rule of holes: when you realize you're in one, stop digging. His second thoughts went into a draft memorandum now in the Royal Archives at Windsor. Getting out, he realized, had been the right course all along, although accomplished now for the wrong reason: defeat. "America is lost!" the king wrote. "Must we fall beneath the blow? Or have we resources to repair the mischief?"

Alternatives to the "Colonial Scheme," he contended, would sustain British power and prosperity while involving an independent American nation. "A people spread over an immense tract of fertile land, industrious because free, and rich because industrious, presently [will] become a market for the Manufactures and Commerce of the Mother Country." He conceded that the war had been "mischievous to Britain, because it created an expence of blood and treasure worth more . . . than we received from America." The more potent Americans became, the less they would be "fit instruments to preserve British power and consequence." Investing any effort to regain hegemony over the colonies would only contribute to "the insecurity of our power." Was an empire destined to be lost worth the price to preserve it? Through the global marketplace the lost lands could still promote British prosperity. Getting out, even accepting humiliation, he argued, could be an unforeseen boon if exploited wisely.

The king's document, based on the thwarted American experience, was a remarkable prophecy. Yet George conceded that the catastrophe had so weakened him at home that he had no clout with his ministers, reactionary or radical. He put the draft aside. Future governments would pour vast resources into subjugating, yet failing to assimilate, the successor jewel in the Crown—the subcontinent of

India—and millions of square miles of indigestible Africa, eventually to relinquish them all at staggering cost to the home islands. It was always foolhardy to be tempted to stay, and always too late to get out. "Mutual interest," the Reverend Tucker had opined, was "the only Tie . . . in all Times and Seasons, and this Principle will hold good, I will be bold to say, till the end of Time."

2

America and the Philippines:
The Graceful Withdrawal

STANLEY KARNOW

However much their methods differed, the British, Dutch, and French intended to cling to their colonies forever. But, from its start in 1898, the United States meant to limit its control of the Philippines—and, to that degree, the American-Filipino experience was unusual in the annals of imperialism.

The conquest of the Philippine archipelago was initially masterminded at the swanky Metropolitan Club in Washington by a covert coterie of obdurate men—highbrow senator Henry Cabot Lodge, naval strategist Captain Alfred Mahan, and particularly belligerent Theodore Roosevelt, then assistant secretary of the navy. The conquest of the Philippines was ancillary to their paramount goal of dislodging Spain from Cuba, but they realized that by propelling American power into the Pacific, businessmen could boost their lucrative trade with China and Japan and profit from tapping their thriving markets and rich sources of raw materials.

Pious evangelical clergymen of every denomination and sect

lauded the endeavor as a unique opportunity to raise the "shining cross" of Christ on the hilltops of Asia. Walt Whitman acclaimed America's actions for expanding the country's horizons, and Rudyard Kipling composed his famous poem "The White Man's Burden" as an appeal to the United States to share with Britain the strenuous, unrequited task of improving the blighted condition of ignorant pagans. The opponents of America's new role in the Philippines included civil service reformer and former senator Carl Schurz, steel tycoon Andrew Carnegie, and onetime patrician New York, Boston, and Philadelphia abolitionists, who equated the subjugation of peoples overseas with slavery and argued that annexation of the islands would blatantly transgress America's lofty principles of "justice" as well as trigger an influx of "barbarous Asiatics" into the country.

Conquering the "Little Brown Brothers"

At dawn on May 1, 1898, obedient to Roosevelt's clandestine orders, Commodore George Dewey steered his minuscule squadron into Manila Bay—and, within seven hours, sank the Spanish ships gathered there. "One of the most remarkable naval battles of the ages," Dewey later proclaimed. Reality was a very different story. Most of the forty Spanish naval vessels in the Manila area were gunboats and other small craft of no consequence. The battle with Admiral Patricio Montojo y Pasarón, the Spanish naval commander in Manila, was a rout. Two hours after the fighting began Montojo lost his flagship, and by the time the Spanish hoisted a white flag, only one of his antiquated ships remained afloat. Nonetheless, the heroic triumph immortalized Dewey. Soon an American infantry brigade entrenched itself on the outskirts of Manila and plunged President William McKinley into a quandary.

Unable to identify the Philippines on a map, he was spoofed by Peter Finley Dunne for not knowing whether they were "islands or canned goods," but McKinley famously explained that after nights of pacing the White House and kneeling to God for help, he decided to "take them all and uplift and civilize and Christianize them." Thus Americans supplanted the Spanish—and, as the witticism went, "three centuries in a Catholic convent were replaced by fifty years in Hollywood."

Filipinos opposed to foreign rule challenged the U.S. presence in a bitter guerrilla conflict, termed by Washington the "insurrection"— a euphemism contrived to convey the impression that America was subduing a rebellion against its lawful authority. The struggle dragged on for five years. The atrocities committed by America and graphically reported in *Harper's Weekly* and other publications mortified the public at home—as Vietnam would generations later. Mark Twain, then at the pinnacle of his fame, led an anti-imperialism movement, publishing an essay, "To the Person Sitting in Darkness," urging President McKinley to redesign the flag with "the white stripes painted black and the stars replaced by the skull and cross bones." Hindered by incompetent leaders and wielding antiquated Mausers and Remingtons, the ragtag Filipino militiamen were no match for the American forces, with their array of Gatling machine guns and Krag-Jørgensen carbines. They lost some 20,000 men—five times the U.S. toll. But the United States still paid a heavy price. By the time the war ended officially on July 2, 1902, it had cost America some $4 billion in today's currency and 4,234 American dead and 2,818 wounded

As many as 300,000 civilians perished, either caught in the crossfire or in cholera and typhus epidemics. A gruesome episode occurred in September 1901 on the Visayan island of Samar after guerrillas slaughtered thirty-seven Americans in the town of Balangiga. The U.S. commander, General Jacob H. "Hell-Roaring Jake" Smith (nicknamed for his booming voice), a veteran of the Civil War and Indian campaigns, declared, "I want no prisoners. I wish you to kill and burn, the more you kill and burn the better you will please me. I want all persons killed who are capable of bearing arms in actual hostilities against the United States." When asked to declare who those persons were, Smith announced they were people ten years and older. Smith's wishes were carried out. Samar was made into a "howling wilderness." A court-martial indicted Smith for butchering two hundred Filipinos, but, like Lieutenant William Calley, who perpetrated the notorious massacre of the Vietnamese My Lai villagers in 1968, Smith was treated leniently. Although he was passed over for promotion to commandant of the Marine Corps, he became a major general following his service in the Philippines, and in the eyes of the military he was regarded as a hero and cheered on his return to San Francisco in 1902.

Appointed governor, future president of the United States William Howard Taft arrived in June 1904 and engaged the prominent architects and urban planners Daniel Burnham and William Parson to transform Manila into a clone of an American metropolis. They laid out mosaic plazas, verdant parks, and capacious boulevards, their titles honoring Alexander Graham Bell, Thomas Jefferson, and Abraham Lincoln, and designed civic buildings with Hellenic columns to replicate those of Washington, D.C. Taft pursued a policy of "benevolent assimilation," the concept vaguely espoused by McKinley. Reflecting the racist attitudes of the time, he regarded Filipinos as inferior. Yet, condescendingly captioning them "little brown brothers," he cultivated the elite *illustrados*, as other U.S. presidents would subsequently, and launched a political tutelage program to prepare them for freedom.

The Philippines Americanized

By 1902 Filipinos elected a parliament, and before long the nation's bureaucracy was almost entirely indigenous. Dispatched to Washington, the astute, debonair Manuel Luis Quezon y Molina vigorously lobbied Capitol Hill on behalf of the Philippines, becoming a familiar figure in its marble corridors and smoky cloak rooms. Quezon even drafted much of the relevant legislation. As a result of his clout, Filipinos were classified "nationals" and, in contrast to other Asians, granted unchecked entrance into the United States, where hospitals coveted them as doctors and nurses—and do to this day.

The U.S. cultural impact was phenomenal. Precursors of Peace Corps volunteers, intrepid young Americans dubbed Thomasites for the vessel that conveyed them, plunged into the remotest corners of the archipelago to teach English, turning it into the country's lingua franca. Under their aegis children learned to brush their teeth and recite their prayers. High school bands, led by drum majorettes, belted out stirring John Philip Sousa marches at raucous fiestas. Gifted musicians imitated Louis Armstrong, Bix Beiderbecke, and Duke Ellington, and vaudevillians copied Fanny Brice, Al Jolson, and Sophie Tucker. Teenagers with cigar brand monikers such as Benedicto and Bonifacio tagged themselves Bernie and Butch. The passport to success for adolescents was an elegant Ivy League diploma.

The drawback for Filipinos was that in the process of being Americanized they also lost control of their economy. By the 1920s America was buying nearly every ounce of Philippine sugar and coconut oil, and the Philippine economy, now largely shaped to supply the United States, rose and fell as the American economy did. Philippine growth, as the impoverished rice farmers of Luzon learned, was lopsided.

Spurred by President Franklin D. Roosevelt, both chambers of Congress voted in 1934 to create a Philippine Commonwealth pending the declaration of independence a decade afterward. Independence was delayed by the Second World War, during which Filipino and U.S. troops fought together in a series of horrendous battles that ended with the defeat of the Japanese and General Douglas Mac-

Arthur proclaiming, "My country has kept the faith" and brought about "redemption of your soil."

When it came, American withdrawal from the Philippines was graceful. On July 4, 1946, President Harry S Truman formally recognized the independence of the Philippines with a proclamation announcing, "The glorious part taken by the Filipino people in the recent terrible war has unquestionably earned for them the right to celebrate July 4, 1946." Earlier in the day Filipinos had marked their independence with cries of "Kalayaan" (freedom), and Philippine President Manuel Roxas had welcomed the new American ambassador, Paul V. McNutt, with the observation, "Our two countries will be united by the unbreakable bonds of mutual respect and affection—bonds forged in the common struggle in peace and war for the greater happiness and welfare of our two peoples."

Independence was not, however, the end of hard bargaining by the United States in its dealings with the Philippines. In the postwar world America was determined to maintain military bases and economic power in its former commonwealth. The Philippine Trade Act of 1946 insured that the Philippines would be preserved as an agricultural land dependent on America, and in March 1947 the two countries signed a formal agreement that gave the United States ninety-nine-year leases on twenty-two Philippine sites, including Clark Field and Subic Bay, plus jurisdiction over the Filipinos working on American bases. It was the best the Philippine government, devastated by wartime losses amounting to $5 billion in today's terms, could manage, but the result was that the Philippines got an economic shot in the arm that no other country was in a position to provide. They also got an America that in the coming decades intimately involved itself in Philippine life, helping to defeat the Huk guerrilla movement in the 1950s, elect President Ramon Magsaysay in 1953, and make Corazón Aquino's succession to power in 1986 an orderly one by encouraging strongman President Ferdinand Marcos to come to America rather than engage in a bloody civil war to stay in power.

Dismayed by the corruption and mismanagement that scourge the islands, many Filipinos look back nostalgically on the American era as utopian. Some politicians even bluster openly that they were CIA "assets." The populace overwhelmingly endorsed the presence of the U.S. bases at Angeles and Subic Bay, though under pressure from powerful factions determined to end what Filipino senator Teofisto "Tito" Guingona called "the last shackles of the past," they were closed by the Pentagon during the 1980s.

In the end, perhaps the best assessment of America's role in the Philippines is that of America's Vietnam foe Ho Chi Minh, who once remarked, "If the French had governed Vietnam the way the Americans administered the Philippines, our struggle against them would have been unnecessary."

3

India and Britain:

The Consequences of Leaving Too Soon

RAJEEV BHARGAVA

SCHOLARLY writing explains British withdrawal from India in terms of a crisis of the colonial state precipitated by Britain's expansive involvement in the Second World War and the sustained anticolonial struggle of Indians led by leaders such as Mohandas Gandhi and Jawaharlal Nehru. This is not a complete explanation, but at least it nudges us in the right direction.

However, crucial questions remain unanswered. Why was the British departure moved up by more than a year—from June 1948 to August 1947? What explains the timing of the withdrawal? What were its moral costs? Could displacement have been averted and the mass killings prevented if withdrawal had been delayed? Did the political actors making these decisions foresee the looming moral disaster? Did the British have information about the extent and depth of violence once they announced the decision that the country would be partitioned? If they had adequate intelligence reports, what measures were taken to quell the violence? And finally, what lessons can be learned from the calamity that followed, during which an estimated one million people died and millions more were displaced? Here, I focus on these questions and limit myself to the period immediately prior to independence.

Let me at the outset state two truisms. *First*, no imperial power has been known to withdraw from a colony without securing its strategic interests. *Second*, an occupying power never leaves with egg on its face and must appear, at the very least, to exit on its own terms.

By the end of the Second World War, Britain knew that its exit from India was imminent. But the formal end of the empire did not mean that the British were prepared to relinquish substantive control over the region, and this consideration was to have a significant impact on the future. Fearful of burgeoning Russian influence in the area between Turkey and India, and worried that the Indian National Congress might be susceptible to such influence, Britain felt that a concessive stance toward the demand for a separate state of Pakistan would better protect British interests in the subcontinent. This tacit support for a new state served another purpose. It helped Britain to save face—to tell the world that it did not leave as a defeated power, with empty hands. Imperial self-esteem depended on the belief that the jewel was still somewhere in the crown. A divided, somewhat weaker subcontinent, with a potentially malleable Pakistan, helped sustain that belief.

The process of cementing a "two-state" solution to "the Hindu-Muslim problem" partly determined the timing of withdrawal, but several other factors also contributed toward it. For one, American pressure on Britain—dictated by similar neo-imperial considerations but also by the United States' own past struggle for independence—made some difference. Winston Churchill's surprising defeat in the postwar elections seemed to have tilted domestic opinion away from those less favorably disposed to Indian independence. A Conservative Party in power probably would have delayed withdrawal, but the Labour Party hesitated less because independence rang true to its own values. Personal ambitions affected smaller but no less important details. Stanley Wolpert has argued that Viceroy Louis Mountbatten's strong disposition toward a speedy withdrawal was not entirely unrelated to his own professionally motivated desire to leave India.

Perhaps another important cause of the timing of withdrawal was that once the decision to have two independent nation-states was announced, overall conditions in the entire region began to deteriorate rapidly. Unwilling to take responsibility for tackling the demons emerging in the subcontinent, Britain was keen to quit as soon as possible. As Sucheta Mahajan has noted, many British officials were happy to "pack their bags and leave the Indians to stew in their own juice."

But what of the Indian leadership? What made Congress Party leaders accept the timing and the potentially costly and immoral outcome of the British withdrawal? Why did Indian leaders acquiesce to the withdrawal at a time when the fear of collective violence was so pervasive? For some, economic reasons are crucial here. Business was declining, the manufacturing sector was affected by strikes, and landlords feared impending peasant uprisings. Under these conditions, both the Indian bourgeoisie and the landlords were eager to see a government more amenable to their influence. There is a grain of truth here, but this explanation is too general and misses the nuts and bolts of what we are after.

Perhaps the most important reason for the hasty transfer of power and the relative insensitivity to its outcome was a substantive change in the structure of power within the Congress Party that brought Nehru and Sardar Vallabhbhai Patel to center stage and severely marginalized Gandhi. As the future wielders of power turned to issues of real politics, ethical considerations were steadily minimized. This is

---

not a criticism of Nehru and Patel. Handling public power is difficult at the best of times. In times of transition, this difficulty multiplies a hundredfold and makes it tough for even ethically minded politicians to be steady and consistent. Mohammed Ali Jinnah, too, faced this problem. He had initially been against the partition of Punjab and Bengal on the ground that it might lead to large-scale collective violence, but as the prospect of power neared, these fears receded. Gandhi's distaste for power continuously and uninterruptedly made him morally sensitive. His presence in the political process at this time of transition would have been vital, but it was not to be, and this had profound and tragic consequences.

Focus on the ethical dimension of political actions requires—especially during moments of transition—uncluttered thinking, not gut reactions. Here the Congress leadership faltered, handicapped by a simplistic belief that a direct and clear announcement of partition would help reduce communal violence. Congress leaders thought that anxiety and uncertainty about the future in the minds of ordinary people lay at the heart of intercommunal violence. A definitive announcement by the government and the leaders of the Congress Party would set minds at rest, and violence would automatically abate.

This proved to be wishful thinking at its worst. How on earth could a simple announcement avert violence? In a state carved out along ethnoreligious lines from a country where Hindus, Muslims, and Sikhs had lived cheek by jowl for centuries, how could freshly invented minorities live without fear amid newly created majorities? A peaceful transfer of population was impossible unless the population was already segregated. The view of the Congress Party leaders betrays an overly rationalist approach that failed utterly to comprehend the depth, complexity, and intensity of emotions unleashed by escalating uncertainty.

It is true, of course, that the primary concern at such times is life itself, but fear that one might die is not the only emotion that grips potential victims. There is the pain of losing a home, which is not the same as loss of material property. There is love, and attachment, for the city or village in which one has grown up—again, not translatable into security of livelihood and property. And, finally, there is resentment at the unfairness of being forced out of a place where one has lived for as long as anyone can remember and being cut off from one's ancestors—for some, a violation of what is most sacred. The complex chain of emotions triggered by the prospect of displacement and dispossession brought many to the brink of violence and barbarism.

The British government and the Congress Party framed the issue in terms of episodic communal violence—an outsider's perspective that hardly got to the heart of the matter. Neither had anticipated the spiraling violence sparked by mutual fear. Assurances from the state about safety and security could not match the horror of seeing friends mutate into murderers. What was urgently needed here was not a view from nowhere—a reasonable, statist viewpoint—but an insider's perspective, which might have made it possible to foresee the brewing storm that would soon wreak destruction on a monumental scale.

Manufacturing the Political Machinery of Violence

How *could* anyone have failed to predict this outcome? The multilayered, wishful thinking of the Congress Party needs to be probed. One cannot make a plausible and persistent claim for independence and then, when push comes to shove, not back it with self-confidence. In normal circumstances—when there are reasonable prospects for peace, when the economy is on the upswing, and when one already has a fairly long experience of administration—effective governance by first-timers is not that difficult. However, when communal disturbances occur daily, the economy is completely destabilized, and there is palpable danger of civil war, one must take a giant leap of faith. One needs to show a tremendous belief in oneself and do so despite (or precisely because of) the uncertainty and lack of assurance from which one might also suffer. How could Congress afford to appear to lose nerve precisely when nerve was most required? Insisting that the situation was under its control was not just an external imperative but a crucial internal requirement. The more pushed to the wall it was, the more loudly its leaders had to say that things were or could be brought under control without any external help. Alas, the scale of the violence was to be so huge and the reality on the ground so bleak that any assertion that the situation could be managed was bound to be proved false immediately. It is surprising that Nehru was not hailed as a tragic hero during the process of partition.

A third reason why the Indian leadership accepted early British withdrawal was a mistrust of the British readiness and ability to stem intercommunal violence. Every Congress leader concurred with Nehru and Patel on this. Gandhi, too, had scant faith in the British. At a prayer meeting, Gandhi famously said that "it was not for the British to give India freedom. They could only get off our backs. That they are under a promise to do. But, for keeping it and giving it shape, we have to look to ourselves." He added that in his opinion, "we are unable to think coherently whilst the British Power is still functioning in India. Its function is not to change the map of India. All it has to do is to withdraw and leave India, if possible, carrying on in an orderly manner, but withdraw in any case on or before the promised date, maybe even in chaos." Gandhi continued to believe that a joint statement from the Congress Party and the Muslim League would halt the violence.

This mistrust in the ability of the British to handle the situation was not ill-founded considering the previous experience of riot management in Calcutta and Bihar. In Bengal during the Great Calcutta

Killings, the government showed a complete lack of will to curb the violence. This connects with another issue. Did the British envisage the violence and the other consequences of their withdrawal?

Some writers suggest that Mountbatten did not have adequate intelligence reports of the scale and intensity of the violence. Others insist that he possessed requisite information to take preemptive action. However, everyone agrees that nobody anticipated the exodus of population—a massive cognitive failure. The British were unable to analyze the dimensions of the problem. It is true that many people, including Jinnah, imagined that only a minimal transfer of population was in the offing. But once widespread violence erupted, it was hard not to conclude that the two states were viable only when populations were ethnically segregated. This triggered fresh rounds of violence when people realized that the only way to ensure separate living was physically to remove the "other" from the neighborhood, even by eliminating him. More compassionate neighbors pleaded with friends to leave. Those gripped by anger and revenge turned to arson and brutal murder. Everything moved rapidly. Everyone became the "other." All were unwitting cogs in a political machinery of violence.

But this argument does not fully wash. Though they had the ability to analyze at least some of the dimensions of the problem, the British appeared not to have put their mind to it. While the Labour government under Clement Attlee was gearing up for withdrawal and justifying its action as the only way of arriving at a workable solution, other voices in Britain and inside the British Parliament warned of the grave consequences of withdrawing much before the June 1948 deadline. Whatever his motivation, Churchill warned that an immediate withdrawal from the subcontinent would leave behind a legacy of war and devastation. Indeed, Churchill stressed the moral responsibility of the British Empire in helping to shape a stable and violence-free dominion. To suggest that the British were not able to foresee the impending violence is to exonerate them, when a large body of written exchanges among British officials suggests the opposite.

Of course, the moral responsibility for anticipating large-scale destruction and displacement lay both with the government and with Indian leaders. Even so, one crucial difference remains. The government had both the intelligence and the resources to understand the complex situation on the ground. The Indian leadership had neither the resources nor the requisite experience to handle it. True, Congress leaders knew of the existence of private armies of political parties, hell-bent on creating unrest through planned and systematic onslaught. But the scale of the violence and the extent of damage by the organized groups could not be assessed by them—and there is nothing to suggest that the intelligence reports available to the British were shared with the Indians. Therefore, the responsibility of the British government to avert violence was far greater. It alone had the power to take preventive measures.

Responsibilities, Ethical and Strategic

If the British had a sense of the coming violence, what preventive steps were taken, and were those steps the best they could do at that time? While the assurances from Mountbatten would suggest that the British were in a position to handle any situation, the reality was far from so. There appears to have been a huge gap between British rhetoric and the effective steps that were actually taken. This was evident in Mountbatten's dealing with the situation in Punjab. He decided not to implement martial law in the region and overall showed an attitude of resignation. On other occasions, he made some bizarre suggestions: if necessary, he said, even tanks and planes could be used to contain violence in the "rabbit warrens of the towns." Even the steps actually taken on the ground seemed ineffective; they were essentially dependent on the strength of the newly constituted Boundary Force, which was ill-equipped in both manpower and resources.

Overall, it is fair to conclude that the British administration did not plan for a breakdown of civil authority; nor did it acknowledge that the Indian Civil Service in 1947 was in a tangle. Around 55 percent of the elite service were retiring, uncommitted, or on the move. As Robin Jeffrey has shown, this was not considered by the British as an important problem to be addressed at the time of partition.

Finally, we must question whether the decisions of imperial powers on withdrawal can ever be based not just on specific strategic and political interests but also on a sense of moral responsibility for their (former) colony. On the evidence of the British withdrawal from the Indian subcontinent, it would be foolhardy to expect any imperial power to be collectively guided by morality. There might be individual cases of morally praiseworthy action, but it is hard to imagine that a system of power based on an ideology of occupation, exploitation, and superiority would incorporate moral considerations. Under the circumstances, it is left for the colonized people and their leaders to be cautious and perceptive in their understanding of the "real" and "actual" interests of the imperial power while negotiations for withdrawal are under way.

4

The Surprising Success:
The United States and Korea

FRED SMOLER

A NY close analogy between "getting out" of Korea and American withdrawal from Vietnam, French withdrawal from Algeria, or British withdrawal from India necessarily fails, because in the sense implied by those cases the United States has not gotten out of Korea. About 27,000 U.S. troops are still stationed in South Korea, down from the 37,500 deployed there in 2004, when the United States and Republic of Korea (ROK) agreed to reduce the American deployment to 25,000 by 2008. So we are still in Korea, and likely to remain there for some time.

The reductions to date of American troops have never been described as a process intended to culminate in the withdrawal of all troops by a date certain, and their pace was for many years uneven. At the height of their wartime strength U.S. forces in Korea numbered 326,363, in the year following the Armistice 225,590, and in 1955 the United States maintained a garrison of 75,328. After that the numbers seesawed, in part according to the level of perceived threat.

In 1956 there were 46,024 American troops in the ROK, by 1964 they had increased by almost a third to 62,596, and they reached 66,531.

While there are some suggestive benchmarks—for example, the 20,000 U.S. troops withdrawn in 1971, under the Nixon Doctrine, or Congress's adoption of the Nunn-Warner Amendment to the 1989 Defense Appropriation Bill, which mandated a reduction in troop strength from 43,000 to 36,000 by the end of 1991—one cannot easily select a moment when the United States decided that it would never again have to fight in Korea. Leaving aside provocations—the occasional murder, kidnapping, and torture of American soldiers and sailors, any of which might have triggered renewed fighting—there were for many decades concerns that an inadequate American garrison would expose South Korea to very rapid defeat by a North Korean (DPRK) military both more numerous and better equipped than the army the ROK then possessed. The U.S. would then have again been compelled to make an ugly choice between acquiescence in a conquest, first use of nuclear weapons, or an immensely difficult re-invasion of the Korean peninsula.

Those were the choices that the United States came very close to facing in both 1950 and 1951, first when following their invasion on June 25 DPRK forces almost effortlessly shattered the ROK army and drove a U.S. intervention force into the Pusan perimeter, then again when the Chinese People's Liberation Army crossed the Yalu River, advanced more than a hundred miles, forced the naval evacuation of the survivors of the U.S. X Corps, and appeared poised to drive the remainder of the U.S. Eighth Army into the sea.

Only recently has the deterrent power of the ROK military come to seem fairly persuasive, and even now the U.S. will be in command of all forces in South Korea in wartime, although the ROK may take over that responsibility in 2009. The resulting situation is the opposite of that in the nearby Philippines, where there is a constitutional ban on foreign military bases and American troops are explicitly banned from joining Filipino troops on combat patrols or operations (although there are allegations that this ban has not been consistently enforced). The United States retains its obligation to defend South Korea in the event of attack by DPRK forces said to number around 1.2 million troops, and which may now possess nuclear weapons. These considerations suggest that the question of how the United States got out of Korea comes down to how the United States secured the Armistice of 1953, an agreement that suspended protracted and large-scale warfare on the peninsula.

From Getting Out to Getting Stuck

There were attempts to get out of Korea before the Armistice of July 1953, indeed before the Korean War even began. U.S. forces landed on September 8, 1945, but U.S. combat units had long been withdrawn by June 25, 1950, the date of the North Korean invasion, and on January 12 of that year Secretary of State Dean Acheson seemed to exclude the ROK from the American defense perimeter. South Korea was supposed to be able to defend itself from a DPRK army that was both thrice the size of its own force and also much-better equipped and trained (DPRK armor was not only technically superior but more than three times as numerous as the ROK's tank force, while DPRK combat aircraft were more than ten times as numerous as the ROK's, which numbered fourteen planes). This initial and twofold attempt to get out of Korea (a refusal to station a deterrent force, and a parallel refusal to promise aid in the event of invasion) was famously a catastrophic failure in two senses of that phrase.

It was also very far from the last attempt to get the United States out of Korea. On June 27, 1950, President Harry S Truman sent a message to Stalin, hoping to secure North Korean withdrawal to the 38th parallel. This action would have preempted American forces getting back into Korea on the scale that subsequently occurred, but the offer was rebuffed. American allies and neutrals also attempted to secure various terms for an American withdrawal, some of which, had they been accepted by the Communist powers, would almost certainly have been rejected by the U.S.: in early July, Britain linked North Korean withdrawal to the 38th parallel to U.S. withdrawal from the Taiwan Strait and the admission of Mao's China to the UN, and India also proposed a deal (China's admission to the UN, North Korean forces' withdrawal, and creation of a 'united and independent' Korea under UN auspices). These offers, which would have limited the scale on which America got back into Korea, were rebuffed.

The subsequent course of the war saw the North Korean offensive halted at the Pusan perimeter, and on October 15, 1950, General Douglas MacArthur's very risky but brilliantly successful invasion at Inchon, which in combination with a drive by the U.S. forces deployed farther south destroyed the DPRK invasion force—around 415,000 had initially crossed the 38th parallel on June 25, and perhaps 25,000 survived to flee back across the parallel in late October.

At this point the United States could in all likelihood have secured partition at the 38th parallel—there was renewed Soviet interest in this solution—and subsequently at the 39th or even 40th parallels, but this solution did not seem an entirely attractive prospect, because North Korea would have very likely revived as a military threat to the ROK, thus pinning significant number of American troops in Korea (which is what eventually happened). In the fall and early winter of 1950, forcible reunification of almost all of Korea under an anti-Communist government seemed both more than feasible and a much more attractive prospect, and at the time possessed the (almost certainly illusory) appeal of possibly wedging China away from a humiliated Stalin.

The main problem with this strategy was that an advance to the Yalu was so likely to threaten the People's Republic of China that it would drive Mao even closer to Stalin. It did. MacArthur's subsequent advance to very near the Chinese border was notoriously followed by massive Chinese intervention, culminating in a successful surprise counteroffensive, one that drove the UN forces back 120 miles, and initially seemed likely to drive the Western intervention force (most of it American) off the Korean peninsula. This setback would admittedly have gotten the Americans out of Korea, although probably into a nuclear war with China. But the Western intervention force stabilized its lines, drove the Chinese back across the 38th parallel, and in several crucial, although now almost-forgotten battles, crushed a series of subsequent Chinese offensives. At this point both sides began to negotiate an armistice—a process that stretched out over two years.

In the end the terms finally agreed upon in the Armistice of 1953 were very close to the terms the UN first proposed in July 1951. Documents released from former Soviet archives suggest that at some periods during the negotiations, time was lost because the Chinese and North Koreans were negotiating in bad faith: after the UN forces crushed the Chinese offensive, the Chinese needed time to stabilize their line and bring up new troops for renewed attacks. In this sense, the halt to UN operations probably cost the future South Korea some territory; it is likely that had UN forces kept pushing north of the 38th parallel in summer 1951 and stopped on a defensible line, they would have been able to hold most of such a line, just as they managed to hold most of the position where they in fact stopped in July.

While several issues separated the Americans and Chinese negotiators—for example, the question whether the Armistice line would be the indefensible 38th parallel or the much more defensible line between the armies at the time of the truce—the most contentious question separating the two sides was the repatriation of POWs. Wars traditionally end with an exchange of all prisoners held by all belligerents, and under normal conditions prisoners are eager to be repatriated. In Korea, however, this was not the case. Many of the prisoners held by the UN were former Nationalist Chinese soldiers unwilling to return to Mao's China, and others were South Koreans conscripted into the North Korean army, similarly unwilling to return to Kim Il Sung's Democratic People's Republic of Korea.

For a number of reasons, the United States refused to agree to forcible repatriation. Although not the most important factor, tactical and strategic calculation did have a role in this refusal. The UN held many more prisoners than did the Chinese and North Koreans (169,000 as opposed to a claimed total of 11,559, one-sixth of the number the Communists had previously claimed to have captured, and only one-ninth of the UN force missing in action). Repatriation of all prisoners would have conferred a significant military advantage on the Communist armies in the event that the Armistice collapsed. In the long run, a considerable number of the soldiers the United States might face in a future European war were also imagined to be unwilling conscripts, and the precedent that defectors would not be surrendered might confer a real advantage in a hypothetical future conflict.

But more than any of these factors, President Truman's moral convictions carried the day. Having agreed to forcible repatriation of Soviet POWs after World War II, he had come to detest returning unwilling men to vicious tyrannies, and his refusal to do something he thought odious was the deciding factor. For the Communist powers, the possible revelation that a significant number of their soldiers apparently considered themselves prisoners within their own societies, men who had made their escape by surrendering, was an enraging and threatening vision, and initially unacceptable.

Crucial to breaking this impasse, as recent revelations from Soviet archives and Chinese memoirs show, was Stalin's death. Stalin died on March 5, 1953, and within two weeks—on March 19—the new Soviet collective leadership told the Chinese and North Koreans to make the deal that was swiftly struck. Within a very short time, the armistice line became the defensible line the Americans had demanded, and there was no forcible repatriation of prisoners.

While the Armistice required many things, what it required above all was Soviet acquiescence, and Soviet acquiescence required Stalin's death. Stalin had armed both the Chinese and the Koreans, who were incapable of arming themselves on a scale adequate to contend with Western armies, while his MiG jets (and sometimes his pilots) had defended them against devastating American airpower. In the long run, fighting without Soviet support would have been impossible. There is in addition some evidence that the Chinese had wearied of the war, while Stalin never did. He did not want North Korea conquered, but once it became clear that the UN forces no longer meditated such an end, Stalin thought he had much to gain from protracting the war, which exacerbated strains between Americans and Europeans, tied down American forces that could have otherwise deployed to Europe, where they would have eroded the Soviet military advantage there, bled the Americans, and bought time for Soviet and Eastern European rearmament.

A War of Adaptation

The armistice had other prerequisites. Above all, it required the crushing defeat of the Chinese military on the battlefield in the summer of 1951; there had been no serious Communist interest in an armistice when either the North Koreans or the Chinese were advancing. Their defeat had occurred in several stages, but the indispensable one was the smashing of the Chinese Spring Offensive, also known as the Fifth Phase Offensive, which had aimed to regain the initiative on the battlefield after the successful UN counteroffensive in March 1951 brought UN forces back to the 38th parallel. The armistice actually achieved also required, however, a demonstration of Chinese ability to defend most of what became North Korea, or at least to inflict serious casualties on any UN offensives that sought to recover any large amount of territory north of the parallel, or else the Americans would have more seriously considered again fighting their way north.

It is tempting to see the dramatic advances and retreats of the seesawing Communist and UN forces as classic examples of successive offensives reaching their inevitable culminating points, each in turn necessarily outrunning supplies and reinforcements and collapsing in the face of predictable counterattacks, with the military balance stabilizing at what became the armistice line. Some accounts of the war have stressed this kind of Clausewitzian rhythm, but the armies fighting in Korea were not the roughly comparable types of antagonist such an explanation implies, and the course of the war was instead determined by successive examples of adaptation to the suddenly revealed capabilities of adversaries neither side had previously encountered.

The Americans, the North Koreans, and finally the Chinese serially underestimated their foes; over the course of the war the Americans and the Chinese in turn learned to counter what had initially seemed insurmountable enemy advantages apparently achieved by a combination of tactical innovation and vast if asymmetrical military resources. The Americans came to understand that Chinese tactics were rigid and repetitive—they generally consisted of first flanking and then pushing an American unit into retreat through prepared ambush positions, and it was in the course of such retreats that Chinese military units inflicted most of the casualties suffered by their opponents.

At the beginning of the retreat from the Yalu, the flanking was achieved in part as a result of MacArthur's recklessly faulty deployments. But this was only the beginning of the story. Still-raw ROK units melted away in the face of the strategic surprise of the massive Chinese army offensive and because of significant Chinese numerical superiority at the first points of contact. The much more heavily equipped American units thus forced to retreat were often road bound, the paths of their retreat could be predicted in advance, and the very lightly equipped Chinese were nimble enough to quite effectively exploit these vulnerabilities. But the same Chinese strengths that had produced the torments of the UN forces during the retreat from the Yalu were inextricably linked to potentially very great weaknesses, and when the shock wore off and General Matthew Ridgeway took over command of the UN forces, those weaknesses were effectively exploited in their turn. Lightly equipped Chinese units fought with what they could carry and could not be readily resupplied. As a result they were soon very short of both food and munitions (the subsequent looting and raping of Korean peasants may well have had a military-political effect of its own), and could not maintain the impetus of their initial attacks. American units with secure flanks could be very effectively resupplied. American units with intact perimeters could be resupplied by air, and American firepower—an American division had as much as twenty times the firepower of a Chinese army division—could inflict horrific losses on Chinese troops caught in the open, a posture almost necessarily assumed by advancing armies (lightly equipped Chinese units by definition lacked adequate anti-aircraft weapons).

Chinese command and control techniques, which to an appalling degree depended on the use of bugles and whistles, had painful limitations when compared to radio nets. The Chinese generals in Korea appreciated these American advantages well before Mao did, and Chinese troops paid a staggering price for Mao's initial inability to appreciate the difference between his new American and his former Nationalist Chinese adversaries. But when in response to apparent overtures for an armistice the Americans allowed the Chinese a breathing space, the Chinese military was able to adapt in turn: it dug in, it moved only at night, and by these means could withstand American firepower to a degree that allowed it to impose a higher price for any renewed UN offensive then the American authorities were at that point willing to pay (President Dwight D. Eisenhower's November 1953 inspection of the strength of the position the Chinese had developed confirmed his decision to abandon any offensive strategy in Korea).

On balance, what has been called Mao's military romanticism proved a much more expensive vice than did MacArthur's hubris. It is a mistake to assume that the stalemate was simply dictated by a military logic that trumped politics; it is more plausible to say that the Chinese and North Koreans retained half of the peninsula because of a series of political decisions made by others.

Miscalculations, and Their Consequences

Despite many contentions to the contrary, agreement by the Koreans on either side was not necessary for the armistice, because that agreement could in neither case be withheld: South Korean President Syngman Rhee sought to sabotage the negotiations, and did manage to slow them down, while North Korea's Kim Il Sung is thought to have been bitterly disappointed by their outcome. But when their backers agreed to stop the war, the war stopped. The willingness of Eisenhower and his secretary of defense John Foster Dulles to significantly escalate the war if an armistice were not forthcoming may have mattered, but recent scholarship suggests that it is hard to measure the degree that it mattered on the evidence of the available documents.

Stalin, who gave Kim Il Sung permission to start the war, and several times kept the war going when he could vary easily have stopped it, was acting on what in retrospect seems a debatable conception of his strategic interest, since the consequences of the protracted war included massive American rearmament, German rearmament, and the transformation of NATO from a meaningless paper coalition to a powerful military alliance—all the reverse of what Stalin had aimed at, as were a number of the war's other results.

Mao also kept the war going for years—without Chinese intervention it would otherwise have ended in the winter of 1950—at least in part out of a calculation of strategic interest, and he too miscalculated, although less grossly than Stalin. Mao won the glory of having stalemated the Americans, but he secured, in addition to the death of a very considerable number of Chinese—one of them his own son—an American commitment to the independence of Taiwan, an American treaty (and military alliance) with Japan, the denial of UN membership for the People's Republic of China for a generation, and the survival of South Korea, again the reverse of the intended results. The protracted war initially deepened and strengthened the ties between China and the Soviet Union, but also produced strains within the Communist bloc and the foreshadowing of the Sino-Soviet split. While the war is often considered a strategic draw, the reasons for this judgment seem elusive; even ignoring the resulting balance of advantage, the war was initiated to destroy the ROK, the United States intervened to preserve the ROK, and the ROK survived.

Truman did not receive the credit for this important achievement in his own lifetime—if he has achieved it yet. The defeat on the Yalu instead destroyed his chance at a second term. What little credit Eisenhower has received for securing an armistice in Korea is probably undeserved: as Stephen Ambrose, arguably Eisenhower's most celebrated (and celebratory) biographer observed, Eisenhower had campaigned for the presidency by attacking a foreign policy he had helped to create and execute (it was also a foreign policy he maintained once in office).

In one view, the cruelest consequence of the war was the victory of Mao's conception of permanent revolution in China, meaning unprecedented surplus mortality on a scale that in most estimates staggers the imagination. But this assumes that without the war Mao's China would have been significantly gentler, which on the comparative evidence seems debatable. So in hindsight the most startling consequence of the war is really the rise of modern South Korea. When the war began, South Korea was one of the poorest societies on earth, and when the war ended it was even poorer: in 1953, South Korean per capita gross national income was $67. In 2008 it was $19,231, and South Korea was the thirteenth largest economy in the world. When the war ended, South Korea was with good reason considered a corrupt and brutal authoritarian regime and would for decades remain so. It is now, of course, a functioning democracy, in some important senses more democratic than the United States was in the middle of the twentieth century. In terms of current catchphrases, this development is something of a puzzlement, for there is no historical and cultural tradition of democracy in South Korea.

The North Koreans, by notorious contrast, live in a famine-wracked tyranny governed with what is even by modern standards extraordinary cruelty. By the lessons often drawn from considerations on how the United States ought to get out of wars (as quickly and completely as possible), and which wars it should avoid (for example, other people's civil wars, or contests with antagonists who might be considered the postcolonial forces of national liberation), the Korean War should have been an unmitigated disaster. Instead the war yielded one of the most startling successes of American foreign policy, achieved not only by stumbling (with no exit strategy) into a fight in Korea, but by staying there for more than half a century.

5

France and Algeria:
Claim Victory and Au Revoir

TODD SHEPARD

I N March 1962, in the eighth year of the Algerian War, the French
government signed off on the Evian Accords, which established
a cease-fire as well as a process that led to the July 5 proclamation
in Algiers of independence—132 years to the day after the Ottoman ruler of that city had surrendered to French invaders. Few people were surprised—indeed, the only surprise was that ending the
French occupation took so long. The end was, after all, inevitable,
or so it can seem in retrospect. But the war was long, and its violence was shocking to contemporaries both in its forms—the French
armed forces' systematic use of torture on suspected nationalists and
the embrace of terrorism by the Algerian National Liberation Front
(Front de Libération Nationale, FLN)—and its effects: the dead numbered some 17,000 French soldiers, about 3,500 French civilians, and
(according to current estimates) between 250,000 and 578,000 Algerians, the vast majority of whom were noncombatants.

Two of the best-known windows into this moment—the on-screen events in Gillo Pontecorvo's film *The Battle of Algiers* and the account and analysis in Frantz Fanon's book *The Wretched of the Earth*—stop in 1961, just before the FLN's final victory. Looking out from the mountaintop, just before the promise of independence has been achieved, gives the undeniable pleasure of being certain of what will happen. Comparing that promise with the ledger of post-independence disappointments (the economic, political, and ideological failures; the still-present threat of terrorist violence; the intense desire of so many North Africans to emigrate to Europe) provides grounds for commentaries, both smug and despairing. Such reflections can seem particularly meaningful because, in today's history books, the Algerian revolution often stands in for the era of decolonization writ large, with the war's exceptional violence magnifying the hopes inspired by "Third World revolutions" as well as the doubts about the West's "civilizing mission." Focusing on how the French withdrawal from Algeria actually happened offers a different perspective.

Skipping over the messy details, it turns out, was an impulse widely shared at the time. Already in early 1962, though few French people could imagine how the Algerian conflict would finally end, they knew that it would. All the better, as most of them had other things to do. In the photo-weekly *Paris-Match*, the year's first editorial, "Snow and Fascism," noted that "between Christmas and these first days of January, 900,000 Parisians put on hold their rendezvous with History and rushed off to the slopes!" In the final months of 1961, French politicians had hesitantly begun to prepare their country for Algerian independence. The minimal coverage the mainstream press now accorded Algeria was occupied by a fierce debate over the merits of splitting Algeria into ministates, one "francophile," one "nationalist," with a third for the Sahara. Left-wing protests drew few into the streets. Algerian civilians as well as French soldiers and nationalist fighters continued to die in what the French government still insisted on calling the "events in Algeria."

On December 29, 1961, President Charles de Gaulle broke this silence in his New Year's address. He told those listening that the year ahead would see the end of French Algeria "one way or another"; 1962, he intoned, "will be the year the army will be regrouped in Europe." The quiescence de Gaulle shattered gave way to an intense period of activity and argument on both sides of the Mediterranean. In Algeria, those who wanted the French to maintain control over their homeland responded with anguish and outraged protest, strikes, and blockades; the most extreme, those who joined the Secret Army Organization (Organisation de l'Armée Secrète, OAS), led by officers who had deserted from the French Army, accelerated their terrorist attacks against suspected FLN sympathizers; random Muslim civilians; and even, occasionally, French soldiers. Working-class neighborhoods in the cities of Algiers and Oran that had remained somewhat mixed, with "Europeans" and "Muslims" living together, were hurriedly and urgently segregated—the exodus of one group or the other driven by pressure from local thugs ("European" and "Muslim") or by fear. In numerous French cities, around Paris and in the provinces, OAS members turned from collecting funds through bank robberies and extortion attempts (a tactic that one angry target, Brigitte Bardot, loudly brought to public attention in late 1961) to a bombing campaign that targeted left-wingers. Terrorist attacks on French civilians succeeded—in ways that reports of officially sanctioned torture, obscene numbers of civilian deaths, and international reprobation never had—in mobilizing the forces of the French left. Hundreds of thousands marched on February 13, 1962, to protest the government's violent response to an anti-OAS rally. These were the months when the "Algerian events" no longer appeared as a fight between the French government and the FLN but were seen as between two visions of France, (in the shorthand of the left) the "Republic" and the "fascists."

It was in this context that the government announced the Evian

Accords. There was loud criticism, but almost all of it came from the very small number of ultras, who still insisted that Algeria remain French. The usual critics of de Gaulle's government, among Communist and Socialist politicians, public intellectuals, or far-left militants, had little to say, except to complain that peace had not come earlier. Focused on the OAS menace to France, they paid little attention to the details of their government's plan for getting out of Algeria.

Leaving for the Wrong Reasons

Officials had organized their pullout, it soon became clear, on the basis of two wrong-headed assumptions. The authorities were sure that they had done what was necessary to convince the substantial minority of Algerians who still wanted a French Algeria to stay put. However, their plans for how to deal with Algerians eager for independence, the FLN in particular, assumed that they would be able to propagate the illusion that the French had decided on their own to leave Algeria and that, rather than a nationalist victory, the independent state-in-waiting was the result of a French plan. But between April and July 1962, the vast majority of pro-French Algerians fled across the Mediterranean, a mad rush that contemporaries termed "the exodus." In those same months, the provisional authority the French had established gained no traction, although their efforts undercut the authority of those nationalist groups most amenable to cooperating in the transition and discredited individual Algerians who actively cooperated. Subsequently, the intranationalist civil war, which broke out almost as soon as independence was declared, left the most vocally anti-French forces in control. Plans for a pluralist democracy were in tatters.

The most immediate victims were two groups of pro-French Algerians. The most well known were the Europeans, more colloquially named *pieds noirs* (black feet), who made up some one million of Algeria's nine million inhabitants. This was a diverse group, most with family ties to Algeria dating back two or more generations, mainly immigrants from Spain, Italy, and Malta, with smaller numbers coming from mainland France. About 120,000 "Europeans" were Jews, the vast majority with ancient family ties to Algeria, dating in some cases to 600 C.E. With a few wealthy exceptions, these *pieds noirs*, although better off than their Muslim neighbors, were poorer than French people living in Europe. Most were deeply attached to their French citizenship, which laws since 1870 had guaranteed. To keep the *pieds noirs* in Algeria the government had pursued a two-track strategy. First, intense negotiations leading up to the Evian Accords aimed to provide them extensive and ironclad guarantees: in independent Algeria they would be able to hold on to French nationality, to opt for dual citizenship, to use the French language in all public affairs, to have civil questions judged under French law and by French jurists; their representation in local government would be assured, their property rights protected. Second, in December 1961, a measure establishing a special status for "repatriates," aimed specifically at *pieds noirs*, became law. As French archives make clear, officials designed this project with the counterintuitive goal of convincing Algeria's Europeans that, since their right to come to France was guaranteed, they should stay in their North African homeland.

Another group, its outlines a bit less obvious, was made up of a minority of Algeria's Arab or Berber inhabitants (rather than call such people Algerians, official French terminology spoke of "Muslims"). This group of French loyalists came to be called the *harkis*. A *harki* was a man who belonged to one of the many self-defense units or *harkas*, which the French government had organized in its attempts to crush the nationalist uprising. By war's end, the term *harki* encompassed all those—male or female—who had worked with the French and failed to distance themselves effectively and in time. Potentially, this was a lot of people, as the numbers of Algerians who served in French uniform or worked for the French state during the war dwarfed those who had directly supported the FLN or other nationalist groups.

According to the Constitution of the Fifth French Republic, ratified in October 1958, all Algerians were full French citizens, with (legally) the same political rights as their compatriots across the French Republic, whether Parisians, Breton peasants, or Europeans in Algeria. While trying to counter international support of Algerian nationalism, French officials constantly pointed to this fact, highlighting not just Algerian electoral participation, but all the other social and economic reforms that aimed to make life in Algeria better, more modern. Indeed, about 10 percent of all French deputies and senators serving in 1962 were, to use the official terminology, Muslim French citizens from Algeria.

When French officials announced the Evian Accords, they repeatedly affirmed that, as with repatriate status, most of the guarantees they had negotiated for Europeans would remain available to all French citizens from Algeria, including "Muslims." Already in February, officers had received instructions to let their Muslim troops know that "their legitimate interests as soldiers and citizens will be guaranteed." If they wished, they could remain French citizens, stay in or join the French Army, even repatriate to France. More emphatic instructions, however, laid out the generous bonuses they would receive if they demobilized and explained the protections the FLN and French government would provide and the opportunities they would have in the new Algerian military and police forces.

Many *harkis* believed government promises. Most *pieds noirs* did not. Starting on April 21, 1962—the day after soldiers captured the head of the OAS, Raoul Salan, thus deflating *pied noir* fantasies that the OAS's violent methods would triumph—waves of departures began, heading from Algeria to mainland France. No one in France had predicted the exodus of almost all the *pieds noirs*, although some had thought large numbers would leave. The subtitle of a magazine article in the summer of 1962, "From Predictions (400,000 Repatriates in Four Years in 90 Departments [across France]) to Reality (400,000 Repatriates in Four Weeks in Four Departments [around Marseilles])," gives a sense of the distance between the most prescient estimates and what happened.

Unprepared, the government quickly cobbled together a plan that provided some support for every *pied noir* who sought refuge in mainland France. It did so against the headwinds of French opinion, which had come to see the *pieds noirs* as only dubiously French, even un-French (as de Gaulle himself opined in private). Indeed, many French people, quite conveniently, came to see the *pieds noirs* and the violent OAS, which had murdered some 2,000 people, as wholly responsible for the war's horrors (rather than the French themselves, their leaders, and their army). In the end, several hundred *pied noir* civilians died during the French retreat from Algeria, some at the hands of French troops, others killed by Algerian neighbors or by armed bands, FLN or not. Most went through difficult departures and uncomfortable arrivals in the metropole. Many became—and some remain—quite bitter about the hostility they encountered from other French people. The experience of the *harkis* was incomparably worse.

The Exodus

In late May, a journalist reported witnessing a horrifying scene. Two jeeps wheeled up to a ship docked in Oran, full of civilians fleeing to mainland France. Officers jumped from the jeeps and led those huddled in back, a group of *harkis*, onto the docks and up the gangway, as the klaxon announcing imminent departure rang out. Rather than let them board, however, sailors separated them from their army guardians and sent the Algerian men back to the dock. As the ship pulled away, the journalist described, another jeep pulled up; a group of "Arabs" jumped out; the *harkis* were killed, their throats slit as the ship's passengers looked on. Days earlier, in fact, a top secret note of May 23 from de Gaulle's office had ordered officials in Algeria to "cease all initiatives linked to the repatriation of *harkis.*" In mainland France, meanwhile, prefects received instructions to report all "irregular arrivals of Muslims in their department." Several days later, an officer directed that "Muslims" who were "too old, physically handicapped, or too young" as well as "single women" should not be transported. Such people, he explained, "are destined effectively either to live off public charity or, with the young women, to turn to prostitution; all will become deadweights."

Until the exodus began, French politicians and officers endlessly repeated that "Muslims" would have the same rights as "Europeans." When "Muslims" tried to exercise these rights, however, French attitudes changed. While French authorities simply stopped talking about "French Muslims" in their public declarations, among themselves they stopped referring to their legal status as French citizens, "repatriates," and began to refer to them as "refugees"—people who might be aided out of French charity. Popular opinion encouraged such an approach. An editorial entitled "Return of the Harkis," in the left-leaning weekly *France-Observateur*, highlighted the dangerous role they might play in "reconstituting the OAS in certain regions" in France. The article detailed the numerous ways the government could restrict and monitor *harkis'* arrivals and "reported" on numerous clandestine landings of *harkis*, supposedly "controlled by the OAS." On the same page, another editorial described "those [Europeans] who are leaving Algeria" as acting "despite the OAS" and "in fear of the OAS." When it came to the *harkis*, however, *France-Observateur* cautioned, "As normal as it is that France should shelter and protect the lives of the French Army's Muslim soldiers who consider themselves menaced by the FLN, it would be dangerous to allow the return to the metropole of veritable Muslim commandos of the OAS." Almost no Muslims, it is worth noting, participated in subsequent OAS attacks in France; a number of *pieds noirs* did.

In the end, according to official estimates, between 25,000 and 27,000 *harkis* arrived in France by June 1963; in an official 1968 census, 138,000 were living in France. (Many were confined to camps in rural corners of France, where they had been consigned upon arrival; some families remained in these camps into the 1990s.) The number killed in Algeria remains unclear, with estimates ranging from 10,000 to 100,000. What is clear is that many (probably tens of) thousands died, many more were tortured, and that, while this retribution was occurring, French officials in decision-making positions did little to intervene.

This inaction happened in large part because neither military nor civilian officials expected it; nor did they give much credence to reports from French officers on the ground. The reasons were double: a widespread suspicion that such officers were trying to undermine the peace process and an unwillingness to grapple with the fact that neither the Provisional Authority, which the Evian Accords had established, nor the FLN and its allied organizations had much control over what was happening. Government responsibility here is substantial: under direct instructions from de Gaulle, who rejected his advisers' suggestions to the contrary, French officials impeded every FLN effort to assert authority in Algeria. De Gaulle insisted that no action, however symbolic, that might suggest that the FLN had any measure of sovereignty within Algeria was permissible— until a French-run referendum, held on July 1, could legitimate French claims that they had decided to leave Algeria, rather than been forced out. Nationalist leaders were thus in no position to stop the so-called "Martians." In French, of course, the word *mars* means both the month of March and the planet Mars: "Martians" were those who, in March 1962, loudly and often brutally proclaimed their undying (if previously invisible) attachment to the nationalist cause. Scenes reminiscent of some that took place at the liberation of France, killing "collaborators"—the often defenseless *harkis*—or attacking their families, seemed a compelling way to demonstrate such a commitment. For some men whose service to France had lasted a bit too long, striking out at those whose French connections had lasted even longer proved particularly tempting. Ever since, Algerian leaders have called opponents *harkis*, members of the "French camp," in order to reject challenges to their incompetence or their authority.

Even before the post-independence civil war, then, the assumptions guiding the French pullout from Algeria created conditions that invited violence (against the *harkis*) and chaos (the mass exodus), although the evidence is clear that no one on the French side and almost no one among the nationalists planned for or wanted either to occur. French eagerness to get out, which was quite intense among average French people as well as among those on the left who had long called for Algerian independence, gave the French government carte blanche. Where de Gaulle's ministers focused most of their attention, of course, was not on Algeria, or on people from Algeria, but on French politics. But that is another history.

6

Vietnam and the United States:
The Price of Intransigence

FRANCES FITZGERALD

IN the wake of the Tet offensive, on March 31, 1968, President Lyndon Johnson announced a partial halt to the bombing of North Vietnam, initiated peace talks with Hanoi, and declared he would not run for a second term. In that election year, Richard Nixon called for "peace with honor" and defeated Vice President Hubert Humphrey, who could not attack Johnson for waging what had become a hugely unpopular war. Many Americans assumed that peace would come in short order. But, though the peace talks had begun, fighting in Vietnam continued for another seven years. In those years, Nixon gradually withdrew American troops from Vietnam but expanded the war to Cambodia and Laos, and with extensive bombing campaigns wreaked more destruction on the Indochinese than had been visited on them in all the preceding years of war. More than 20,000 American troops died, and upheavals in the United States tore the country apart, creating divisions that remain with us today.

The reason for this was simple: Nixon, as he said, had no intention of becoming "the first president of the United States to lose a war." To him, that meant that he had to sustain the anticommunist government in Saigon at least through his own term in office. On the other hand, the Vietnamese communists, north and south, who had fought a nationalist and a revolutionary struggle against the Japanese, the French, and the Americans since the Second World War, would not abandon their cause.

During the 1968 campaign, Nixon ruled out a U.S. "military victory." The only strategy the military planners had figured out was the attrition of enemy forces, and the Tet offensive had convinced the American public that attrition wasn't working and that the only prospect was for more American casualties with no end in sight. A withdrawal of U.S. troops from Vietnam had thus become a political necessity.

But how to withdraw and maintain the Saigon government? Created by the United States after the French withdrew in 1954, that government, the Republic of Vietnam, never gained political legitimacy. Since the fall of Ngo Dinh Diem to a military junta in 1963, it had been merely an administration and an army held together by American aid, with no politics except anticommunism. Johnson had sent U.S. troops to Vietnam in 1965 because it was disintegrating under political and military pressure from the southern revolutionaries, the National Liberation Front. Later, regular North Vietnamese troops had joined the battle. However, the three years of the American war had taken a toll on the NLF guerrilla forces and driven much of the rural population that supported them into the garrisoned cities and towns. In the Tet offensive, the NLF suffered crippling casualties; the North Vietnamese army was less affected, but it could not undertake a major new offensive soon. Nixon determined to press the military advantage while slowly withdrawing the American troops.

Under the rubric "Vietnamization," Nixon launched a program

of military aid to Saigon that permitted the junta, led by General Nguyen Van Thieu, to draft a million men into its military forces and to acquire the fourth-largest air force in the world. In addition, he initiated the Phoenix program in an effort to eliminate the NLF civilian political cadre through enlarging and centralizing the government's secret police forces. Then, in 1969-1970, the American forces went on the offensive, conducting major sweep-and-destroy operations in central Vietnam, entering the densely populated Mekong Delta for the first time, pursuing local NLF units, and bombing villages with B-52s. In support of these operations, Nixon authorized a secret bombing campaign against NLF and North Vietnamese sanctuaries in Cambodia. The raids, which went on for fourteen months, encouraged Cambodian prime minister Lon Nol to overthrow Prince Norodom Sihanouk, the monarch who had long tried to keep Cambodia out of the war. On April 30, 1970, Nixon announced he had ordered U.S. and ARVN (Army of the Republic of Vietnam) troops into Cambodia to find and destroy the enemy's central command base. The base, as it turned out, had been evacuated weeks before, but the U.S. campaign succeeded in disrupting North Vietnamese supply lines.

By 1971, these military operations and the Vietnamization program had achieved one important U.S. objective: they had destroyed the NLF as an effective military force and given the Saigon government control of most of the population. But the cost was extremely high. U.S. combat units took devastating casualties and morale among the GIs collapsed: drug use became common, racial tensions erupted, individual units refused combat, and officers were murdered by their troops. At home, the antiwar movement grew, and huge demonstrations erupted in cities and on campuses across the country. Not all of them were peaceful, and, sensing a reaction, Nixon and Vice President Spiro Agnew called on "the silent majority" for support against the media and academic "elite" that they blamed for the demonstrations. Passions flared on both sides. After the invasion of Cambodia, over a third of U.S. colleges and universities shut down, and an Ohio National Guard unit, ordered onto the campus of Kent State University, fired on a group of protesting students, killing four of them. Cambodia fell into anarchy, from which the murderous Khmer Rouge emerged.

For Nixon, there remained the problem of the North Vietnamese army. Foreseeing a major offensive in 1972, U.S. commanders in Saigon determined to thwart it by cutting the Ho Chi Minh trail, a network of roads and paths through the mountains of the Laotian panhandle that the North Vietnamese used as their logistical corridor to the south. The Cooper-Church amendment and other congressional measures passed after the Cambodian invasion barred American forces from entering Cambodia and Laos, but the ARVN was not so constrained, and on February 8, 1971, some 30,000 ARVN troops attacked across the border with American air support. The operation was foolishly conceived (the Ho Chi Minh trail could be "cut" only for as long as the ARVN remained as a blocking force) and badly executed. The ARVN units, finding themselves attacked by North Vietnamese artillery and ground troops, began a retreat that soon turned into a disastrous rout—calling the whole Vietnamization program into question.

Peace Almost at Hand

Nixon had always understood that U.S. gains against the NLF were only tactical and temporary. His hope was that he could convince Hanoi to back down by threatening to bomb North Vietnam into extinction—and the bombing of Cambodia was meant to signal his resolve. He also hoped to persuade the major communist powers to bring the North Vietnamese to heel.

Since 1965, the Soviet Union and the People's Republic of China had furnished Hanoi with significant quantities of military aid and with rice to feed its population. Disputes between the two powers had complicated these aid programs. Nixon judged that at some point both countries would develop priorities more important to them than the support of the Vietnamese revolution. To the Soviets, he held out the promise of a strategic nuclear arms agreement and to the Chinese the promise of a rapprochement with the United States. These initiatives had their own rewards—they produced the astonishing spectacle of Richard Nixon and Mao Zedong smiling for the television cameras in Beijing—but they did not persuade either power to abandon Hanoi.

In March 1972, the North Vietnamese launched a major three-pronged offensive, using tanks and heavy artillery for the first time in the war. In all three sectors, the ARVN, though similarly equipped, fled before them. The North Vietnamese advanced so rapidly they outstripped their planning; they hesitated, and B-52 raids pulverized their positions. Their advance was stopped, they took huge casualties, but their offensive permitted the southern revolutionaries to establish new bases and lay the groundwork for a renewed political struggle. An intense U.S. bombing campaign against the North failed to halt their support for that struggle.

By June 1972, there were only 47,000 American troops left in Vietnam, and the time had come for a peace agreement. In secret talks with Secretary of State Henry Kissinger in Paris over the years, the North Vietnamese negotiator, Le Duc Tho, had consistently called for a complete withdrawal of American troops in exchange for a cease-fire and the return of prisoners of war. He had rejected Kissinger's proposal for a "mutual withdrawal," that is, a simultaneous withdrawal of North Vietnamese from the South, and he had insisted on a condition that Nixon found unacceptable: the replacement of the current Saigon regime with a coalition government. But with the new balance of forces in South Vietnam, both sides saw the outlines of an agreement. In a speech on May 8, Nixon promised to pull out all American troops following a cease-fire and the release of prisoners of war; afterward, he said, an internal political settlement could be worked out "by the Vietnamese themselves." Conspicuously, he made no mention of a "mutual withdrawal," thereby removing a major obstacle for the North Vietnamese. After further talks between Kissinger and Tho in Paris, the North Vietnamese, on October 8, issued a nine-point draft agreement that removed a major obstacle for the United States. The draft did not insist that Thieu step down in advance of an armistice; rather, it proposed that the Republic of Vietnam and the Provisional Revolutionary Government (the governmental structure of the NLF) be recognized as "administrative entities" and that they should appoint a council of national reconciliation that would hold democratic elections for a new government. Reunification would take place at an indefinite date in the future through "peaceful means." Meanwhile, military assistance to both sides would be limited to replacements.

Kissinger was elated. With minor modifications, he accepted the draft and made plans to fly to Hanoi in late October to initial the agreement. The formal signing was to take place the following week, just before the U.S. presidential election. In Saigon, however, he found Nguyen Van Thieu adamantly opposed. This was hardly surprising, as Thieu's position had always included "Four Nos": no recognition of the enemy in the South, no neutralization of the South, no coalition government, and no surrender of territory. Kissinger promised Thieu that if the other side violated the agreement, U.S. retaliation would be swift and severe, and went so far as to threaten him with a cutoff of U.S. aid, but Thieu would not budge. Nixon was furious, but, deciding that he couldn't afford to scuttle the Saigon regime or sign a separate peace, he backed down. Dutifully, Kissinger cabled Hanoi and once again raised the issue of North Vietnamese troops in the South. Hanoi responded by publishing the text of the agreement and a history of the secret talks.

Withdrawal and Collapse

In a press conference on October 26, Kissinger acknowledged that the text was essentially correct and said that while certain technical issues remained, the problems were not very great. Peace, he declared, was "at hand." It was not. Returning to Paris on November 19, Kissinger demanded that Tho reopen a number of the major issues and threatened "savage" bombing of the North if he wouldn't. Tho refused and returned to Hanoi. On December 17, Nixon authorized renewed bombing of the North, and for eleven days B-52s and other American aircraft flew 3,000 sorties, mainly over the heavily populated corridor between Hanoi and Haiphong, attacking power plants, shipyards, and other installations that had been off the target list until then. The "Christmas bombing" was the most concentrated air offensive of the war; some thirty American planes were lost, and the public reaction was negative. On January 8, Kissinger and Tho resumed their meetings, and on January 27 the Paris Peace Agreement was signed. Nixon and Kissinger claimed that Hanoi had been bombed back to the negotiating table, but the text of the agreement was essentially the same as the draft Hanoi had published in October. This time, Nixon told Thieu he would sign the agreement without him, and Thieu, reassured that Nixon would bomb the North again if necessary, cooperated.

Once American troops had been withdrawn and prisoners of war exchanged, Thieu launched operations against the zones of enemy control in the Delta and along the Cambodian border. The PRG kept calling for a cease-fire and a political settlement as specified in the agreement. Thieu, however, could not have survived in a political struggle, and the war continued, as Nixon and Kissinger assumed it would. The U.S. Congress rebelled against Nixon's promise to reintervene if the communists violated the truce, and passed bills blocking funds for any U.S. military activities in Indochina. But U.S. military aid to Thieu continued as before.

At the end of 1973, the Thieu government held a strong military position. With a million men under arms, its army controlled most of the country and most of the population. Its difficulties were internal. The American troop presence had pumped billions of dollars into the civilian economy, and U.S. troops had, directly and indirectly, employed hundreds of thousands of people. With the Americans gone, unemployment soared and inflation rates climbed so high that ordinary soldiers could not afford to buy rice for their families. Corruption had always been pervasive, but in the declining economy it gave rise to protests against Thieu and his circle of generals, who were seen as the major war profiteers. ARVN morale plummeted. Two hundred thousand soldiers deserted in 1974. Faced with this crisis, all the American embassy and the White House could think of was to pressure the Congress for more aid to Thieu.

In later years, Kissinger maintained that the Watergate scandal spelled the end for the Saigon government. True, as the scandals were progressively revealed, Congress gradually reasserted its powers over foreign policy, and in August 1974, when Nixon resigned rather than face impeachment, Congress reduced military aid to Saigon from the billion dollars that had been requested to $700 million. But the decrease might have come anyway, given the unpopularity of the war. In any case, the argument raises the question of whether Nixon's aid program would have been enough to save the Thieu regime.

The North Vietnamese spent much of 1973 and 1974 building an all-weather highway network from the demilitarized zone to a base camp north of Saigon. Meanwhile, the leaders in Hanoi debated strategy and timing. In late 1974, it was decided that the commanders in the South could launch attacks in 1975, but should not expect a final victory until 1976 or 1977. A successful attack on a provincial capital in January accelerated the schedule. In early March, North Vietnamese regular divisions attacked across the demilitarized zone and through the central highlands, scattering the ARVN troops as they went. Thieu called for a retreat and ordered the highland divisions back to defend Saigon, but their commander fled and a rout ensued. In the northern sector, Hue fell almost without a fight, and Danang, full of panicked troops and civilians, fell five days later. Once again, the North Vietnamese forces could not keep up with the collapse of the ARVN, but this time they did not hesitate; they moved swiftly on Saigon. On April 29, their lead units entered the city, and the last American helicopter lifted off the roof of the American embassy.

What If?

The war was over, but not the suffering. Since 1969, over a hundred thousand ARVN soldiers and half a million North Vietnamese and NLF troops had died in combat—along with uncounted numbers of civilians. The economy of the country was shattered, the southern cities filled with refugees and former soldiers. Distrustful of the southerners, even those who had worked for the revolution, the North Vietnamese appointed their own officials and moved swiftly to reorganize the society and economy on the model of the North, paying no heed to local conditions and customs. Hundreds of thousands of former government officials, military officers, and members of the intelligentsia were sent to reeducation camps, while millions of the metropolitan jobless were sent to "new economic zones" in the border areas to reclaim poor land with rudimentary tools. A million South Vietnamese fled the country on whatever vessels they could find, and many of them spent years in refugee camps in neighboring countries.

As president, Nixon never promised to win the war. By 1969 there was no reason to believe that it *could* be won. Certainly, as the record shows, both he and Kissinger understood that without American troops and B-52s, a communist victory was at some point inevitable. Had they decided to end the war in 1969 or in any subsequent year, they could surely have prevailed upon the North Vietnamese to give them the "decent interval" between the withdrawal of American troops and a communist victory that Kissinger thought necessary to preserve American credibility in the world and to uphold American honor. The North Vietnamese leaders might have seemed indifferent to the loss of lives and the destruction of their economy, but they were not. They desperately wanted American troops out of Vietnam. Under the threat of a renewed bombing of the North, they would have been willing to wait at least two years with a neutralist coalition government in the South. Such a solution would have been more than acceptable to the southern revolutionaries, who had been almost wiped out, and it would have given the noncommunist South Vietnamese alternate possibilities. Those who wanted to leave the country could have done so in an orderly fashion. Those who stayed could have organized politically—Buddhist and Catholic parties might have emerged—and made an accommodation with the communists, as many had in 1964–1965. Reunification would have come eventually, but the South Vietnamese would have had a voice in determining the future of their country—and all this with far fewer casualties.

7

The Gates of Gaza and the Limits of Power:

Israel and Gaza

SHLOMO AVINERI

THE Gaza Strip is a small, dagger-shaped coastal territory, wedged between Israel and Egypt, 25 miles long and 7.5 miles at its widest, comprising 360 square miles. Home to 1.4 million Palestinians, many of them 1948 refugees or their descendants, it is perhaps the best illustration of the tragic dimensions of the Israeli-Palestinian conflict, as well as of its intractability.

Between World War I and 1948, the area was part of the British Mandate of Palestine, and in 1947 it was allocated in the United Nations partition plan to the Arab state. When Egypt joined other Arab countries in their war against Israel in 1948, the Egyptian army occupied the area, and its few Jewish kibbutzim were overrun and destroyed. With the failure of the Palestinian Arabs to set up a state of their own, Gaza remained under Egyptian military administration. In the 1950s, Egypt tried to establish an "All Palestine Government" in Gaza, headed by the former mufti of Jerusalem, Hajj Amin al-Husseini; but with the other Palestinian territory—the West Bank—

annexed by Jordan, the Gaza government failed to achieve legitimacy, and its ramshackle institutions soon vanished from view.

The Gaza Strip was briefly occupied by Israel (for a couple of months) during the Sinai-Suez War of 1956, but then reverted to Egyptian military rule until 1967, when Israel took control of it in the Six Day War. Its original population was swollen by Palestinian refugees from the 1948 war, and the temporary relief they received through the United Nations Relief and Works Agency (UNRWA) proved to be permanent, perpetuating their existence in the camps and their status as refugees. All through the almost twenty years of Egyptian occupation, Gaza residents were not allowed into Egypt, nor were they granted any political rights. While West Bank Palestinians received Jordanian citizenship and passports, the inhabitants of the Gaza Strip—long-time residents as well as refugees—were left by the Egyptians in a political and legal limbo. Until 1956 there were numerous incursions from the Strip into Israel, followed by Israeli reprisals. The situation was more or less stabilized after Egypt returned to the area in 1957.

On occupying Gaza in 1967, Israel set up a military administration, which was initially viewed as a stopgap measure until a peace agreement would settle Gaza's status. But when no negotiations took place, this provisional structure became semi-permanent, lasting until 1994, when in the wake of the Oslo Accords Israel handed over control to the Palestinian Liberation Organization. Gaza City became one of the seats of the new governing Palestinian Authority under Yasir Arafat (the other being Ramallah in the West Bank).

Gaza Under the Palestinian Authority

The Gaza Strip handed over to the Palestinian Authority was very different from the Strip captured by Israel more than twenty-five years before. First, the population had more than doubled; second, tens of thousands of Gazans, mainly from the refugee camps, who had never been gainfully employed during the decades of Egyptian rule, found work in Israel—mainly in agriculture, construction, and the service industries—bringing modest prosperity to a deracinated and impoverished population. But there were also structural changes that transformed the demography of the Gaza Strip, even if numerically they were marginal: the establishment of Jewish settlements.

Initially, Israel's policy was minimalist and mainly security oriented, aimed at preventing another Egyptian occupation of the area by trying to create a territorial wedge between it and Egypt. Later, temporary military camps were turned into half-military, half-civilian outposts and then eventually "civilianized." With the rise of the nationalist Likud government of Prime Minister Menachem Begin in 1977, all pretense of temporariness was abandoned, and settlement activities were intensified; ultimately more than twenty villages were established, with a population of around nine thousand inhabitants. Despite their small number, they controlled a disproportionate part of the Strip's arable land as well as its scarce water resources.

When Israel handed over the Gaza Strip to the Palestinian Authority, it maintained its control of the settlements. Most of them were concentrated in a contiguous bloc abutting the Egyptian border, but a few were isolated enclaves in the midst of Palestinian-controlled areas. With Israel in control of the settlements and their extensive lands—and also of the numerous roads leading to them, sometimes through densely populated Palestinian areas—the reality of fewer than ten thousand Israelis living in the midst of more than a million Palestinians appeared even more anomalous than before.

The other important shift in the politics of the Gaza Strip between 1967 and 1994 was the emergence of violent Palestinian resistance against Israeli rule, aimed not only against military targets, but also against the civilian population of the settlers. That the settlers developed a thriving agricultural economy, employing thousands of Palestinian workers, only added resentment to the other complexities of the gerrymandered Strip.

Initial Palestinian resistance in the late 1970s was successfully suppressed by the Israeli army, countering Palestinian terrorism with counterinsurgency methods that combined force with sophisticated political manipulation. One of these political schemes led to unexpected and baleful consequences.

In the 1970s and '80s, Palestinian resistance and terrorism in Gaza were mainly organized by the Fatah wing of the PLO, under Arafat, from headquarters in Beirut and later in Tunis. At the height of these activities, some Gaza clerics approached the Israeli military and asked for permission to set up Islamic-oriented schools, clubs, and social services, explaining that they wanted to keep young people off the streets and away from trouble. Because of the legacy of Egyptian rule, there have been historical links between the religious Al-Azhar University in Cairo and a local Gaza branch campus. The Israeli military viewed this as a quietistic alternative to the militant Fatah, especially since the clerics explained that they had only educational aims and occasionally criticized the "godless" Fatah. Israel granted the requests.

This was the beginning of Hamas: what might perhaps have been a short-term smart move in a counterinsurgency policy turned out in the long run to establish a strong social base for Hamas, which eventually developed a fundamentalist, anti-Israeli ideology of jihad.

When Arafat's Palestinian Authority took over Gaza from the Israelis, it found a powerful network of religious organizations, from kindergarten to university, from women's organizations to youth clubs, that opposed the Oslo Accords and became an effective alternative to the PA, ultimately undermining its ability to rule Gaza. Such were the unintended consequences of Israel's—at one time successful—counterterrorism policies of the 1980s.

All this came to a head following the collapse of the Oslo process in 2000, when at Camp David President Bill Clinton failed to achieve an agreement between Israeli Prime Minister Ehud Barak and the PA's Yasser Arafat. The ensuing violence ("the second intifada") toppled the Labor-led government of Barak and brought to power the Likud, headed by Ariel Sharon.

It is here that one of the most momentous and paradoxical watersheds in Israeli politics occurred. Sharon was elected on a hawkish platform, vowing "to end Palestinian terrorism"; he had considerable success in reducing the number of suicide bombers who blew themselves up in the midst of Israeli towns, in supermarkets and schools. But then he began to change course.

The reasons for this were complex and sometimes contradictory. While Israel's major operations against the bases used by the terrorists in the West Bank were successful, they entailed, as in the case of Jenin, massive incursions into areas populated by civilians. These produced severe international criticism—but also internal debates that posed serious ethical challenges to the Israeli army, especially as reserve units with older soldiers were involved in the fighting. Sharon was reported to have said, "Jenin was a success, but we can't do it twice a month."

Yet negotiations with the Palestinian Authority appeared useless, as Arafat lost credibility in Israel: most Israelis believed that after the failure of Camp David in 2000, he had adopted, or at least condoned, terrorist attacks against civilians. Consequently, progress in accordance with the U.S.-sponsored "road map," which envisaged a two-state solution emerging out of Israeli-Palestinian negotiations in three stages over a couple of years, became stuck in mutual recriminations. The damage undermined any realistic hopes for meaningful Israeli-Palestinian negotiations, even after Arafat's death in 2004.

It was this stalemate that prompted Sharon to realize that unless he tried novel approaches, he might find himself confronted by a new U.S.-backed initiative that would put his government—and Israel—under pressure to make unwelcome concessions. The status quo, Sharon knew, was untenable. But beyond this, Sharon concluded that some of his and the Likud's longstanding goals were unrealizable: Israel would not be able to hold on indefinitely to all of the West Bank and Gaza—both because of the almost universal acceptance abroad of a two-state solution (embraced also by a growing number of Israelis), as well as because, if it did hold on, demographics would soon make the Jewish population a minority in its own land. In the area that includes Israel, the West Bank, and Gaza, the Arab population was approaching parity with the Jews and would overtake them within less than a generation. As the Israeli left has been saying for some time, a "Greater Israel" would eventually mean a bi-national state, not a Jewish democratic homeland.

To this was added a worsening situation in the Gaza Strip. If Israel's security policies, including building a fence or wall, were successful in containing suicide bombers and other violent acts against Israeli civilians coming from the West Bank, in Gaza the situation was more complex. The tiny Jewish settler population needed daily protection: school buses and supply vans had to be escorted by armed Israeli convoys; the perimeters of isolated settlements had to be guarded by ever larger military units. At one time, the number of soldiers protecting the settlers was larger than the settler population of 9,000.

Gradually, Sharon began indicating publicly the changes in his thinking. To the chagrin of his own Likud supporters, he argued that "occupation was bad not only for the occupied, but also to the occupiers." He told a Likud conference that "regardless of what we want, eventually a Palestinian state will emerge." Finally, in a major policy statement in December 2003 at the annual Herzliya Security Conference, he set out his new policy: absent meaningful negotiations, Israel should undertake unilateral steps of "disengagement" from certain areas in the occupied territories. On February 3, 2004, in an interview with the daily *Haaretz*, he spelled it out: all the Jewish settlements in the Gaza Strip, and four isolated settlements in the West Bank, would be evacuated. Israel, he said, cannot wait until the Palestinians make up their mind: "We have to start making decisions about our own borders."

This bombshell was Sharon's Gaullist moment; the "Father of the Settlements" had adopted the intellectual framework of the Israeli left, and this caused a political earthquake. In his own party, many vociferously objected to what they saw as a betrayal of Likud's basic ideology. In response, Sharon put his proposals to an internal party referendum—and lost. When he decided to push ahead, ordering the army to prepare operational plans for the disengagement, some of his own cabinet ministers balked; they were dismissed, and others left his party, moving farther to the right. The army chief of staff, who appeared lukewarm about the disengagement, was replaced by a more pliable general. Finally, Sharon decided to abandon Likud altogether and set up a new centrist party, Kadima. He took with him some of Likud's most prominent leaders, such as Ehud Olmert, Tzipi Livni, and Shaul Mofaz; and some Labor leaders, most significantly the former Labor party chairman and prime minister, Shimon Peres. The historical stalemate between doves and hawks appeared to disappear under a new dispensation, which appealed strongly to members of both historical camps. Sharon's rump cabinet continued for some time as a minority government, but eventually he had to call for early elections, more than a year ahead of the planned schedule.

Sharon's Rubicon

This was a total redrawing of the political map of the country. The man who stood for the most hawkish policy—settlements, opposition to a Palestinian state, no withdrawal—became the darling of

Israel's left, while being reviled as a traitor by the settlers and their right-wing supporters. There was fear of an assassination attempt on Sharon's life, and with the memory of Rabin's assassination still fresh, this was taken seriously. And there was considerable concern that the forceful removal of the Gaza settlers might end in violence, perhaps even precipitate a civil war.

Although the number of settlers to be evacuated was relatively small, both the right and the left understood that a Rubicon was about to be crossed. For years it was a mantra of the Israeli right that Jews cannot be evacuated from any area of the Land of Israel. At the same time, people on the left sometimes voiced, in despair, the view that the settlements are irrevocable; no Israeli government would have the political will and ability to evacuate any of them. Now this taboo was about to be breached, and certainly the right understood that once even a few settlements were evacuated, the door would be opened—politically and psychologically—for further disengagements, evacuations, and retreats from the much more numerous settlements on the West Bank.

For months, massive demonstrations against disengagement took place; leaders of the settlement movement and some of their rabbinical supporters threatened civil disobedience, some even calling for soldiers to refuse to carry out orders. In the heated atmosphere, the disengagement was called "ethnic cleansing" and compared with the expulsion of the Jews from Spain in 1492 or even with the Holocaust.

Eventually, between August 15 and 23, 2005, the disengagement took place, peacefully. More than 30,000 soldiers and police officers—all of them unarmed—were involved; the settlers, who until the last moment believed that the evacuation would not take place (perhaps due to divine intervention), did not oppose the army violently, though many had to be dragged from their homes, which were then destroyed by Israeli bulldozers. The pictures of the evacuation, shown live on Israeli television, deeply stirred the nation: even opponents of the settlers could not but be moved by pictures of whole families—including women and children—being forcibly removed from homes in which many had lived for decades, by the country's own army. But the months-long training of the army, instructed to proceed "firmly but compassionately" (*bi-nekhishut u-vi-regishut*) proved a success. Beyond the evacuation itself, the process proved the resilience of the Israeli democratic system, and the policy was supported by a large majority of Israel's population.

The Aftermath

The immediate consequences appeared hopeful, but the long-term results were mixed, sometimes problematical, or worse. At the time of the withdrawal, Israel offered refuge to a few hundred Palestinian Gaza residents who had worked, openly or clandestinely, for Israel or its security services. They were given housing, work opportunities, and other support in Israel, and melted into Israel's Arab population; though many Israeli Arabs, if they recognize the Gazans, view them as traitors and collaborators. Paradoxically, but perhaps not surprisingly, some of the evacuated Jewish settlers have still not been totally reconciled to their fate and occasionally surface angrily and resentfully in Israeli public discourse. They are sometimes cynically used by the opponents of further disengagements. On the eve of the Gaza disengagement, the government offered the evacuees housing as well as generous financial compensation packages. Many of them refused to go through the complex bureaucratic steps necessary to receive the help, some hoping until the last moment that the disengagement would not take place, and some willfully obstructive. As a consequence, a number of families still live in temporary housing and have not yet been adequately compensated for their losses or economically rehabilitated.

But the major consequences of evacuating Gaza were political, and here the jury is still out. After the disengagement, Sharon himself suffered a series of strokes that took him out of political life, and Kadima faced the 2006 elections headed by Sharon's deputy, Ehud Olmert. It did win the elections, but less dramatically than it would have done had Sharon led the party, and Olmert set up his own Kadima-Labor coalition government, committed to further disengagements.

It was not to be. Israel's hope after leaving Gaza was that the Palestinians there, freed from the occupation and the daily disruptions caused by the presence of Jewish settlers in their midst, would now commence on the road of nation-building and reconstruction. Yet the opposite happened: in a rage that sent shudders through the hearts of Israelis who watched it on television, Gaza Palestinians set about destroying the synagogues left behind—as well as the agricultural greenhouses that were supposed to become part of the infrastructure for a revival of the local economy, now under Palestinian control.

Moreover, and more significantly, the political situation in Gaza remained fluid; after a period characterized by a contested election (Hamas won with only 44 percent of the vote) and failed coalition governments, Fatah and Hamas descended into a bloody civil war, culminating in June 2007 in a violent putsch in which Hamas took control of the Gaza Strip from the Palestinian Authority.

While this de facto Hamas government has not been recognized by anyone in the Middle East or elsewhere, it did undermine the logic of Israel's withdrawal from Gaza. Withdrawing without even the framework of an agreement with the PA was always controversial, though it is reasonable to argue that had Israel offered to negotiate the withdrawal, it would still be bogged down in the negotiations and would be in control of the Strip, with the settlements in place. Such speculation can never be verified or falsified.

Yet what is incontrovertible is that the unilateral withdrawal did not achieve its aims. The hoped-for quiet border between Israel and Gaza became a confrontation line, with Hamas and its allies continuously shelling Israel's southern towns and kibbutzim with rockets and mortars. Hamas's incursions into Israel proper culminated in the killing of a number of Israeli soldiers and the capturing of one—Gilead Shalit—whose captivity and disappearance in 2006 epitomize for many Israelis their broken hopes for what they believed could be achieved by the painful dismantling of Jewish settlements in Gaza. It appears that withdrawal did not bring de-escalation: it seemed to empower the more radical groups among the Palestinians and brought the war even nearer to Israel's towns and cities. Nor did the effective blockade imposed by Israel on Gaza—supported actively by Egypt, diplomatically by the United States and the European Union, and implicitly by the PA—succeed either in weakening Hamas's control of the Strip or cutting into its popular support.

Beyond this, however, Israelis view Hamas as a fundamentalist Islamist organization, committed to the destruction of the Jewish state, practicing terrorism and supported by Iran. More than this: it also subscribes to an obnoxious ideology that views the Jews as such—and not just Israelis or "Zionists"—as its enemies. In its charter, which is taught in its schools, a whole chapter (no. 22) is devoted to the Jews, who are seen as responsible for all the calamities of the modern age. In language obviously lifted from *The Protocols of the Elders of Zion*, but also adding some twists of its own, Hamas maintains that the Jews (together with the Masons) instigated both the French and Russian Revolutions, were responsible for World War I (so as to dismantle the Ottoman Caliphate) as well as for World War II (so as to make money out of the fighting). It is not easy to live next door to a political entity committed to such an ideology, or to consider negotiating with it.

When Hamas terminated a fragile six-month truce in the autumn of 2008 and intensified its shelling of Israeli towns in the south,

Israel launched a massive operation against it. Despite the ferocity of the attack, it failed to dislodge Hamas or fully stop its shelling of civilian targets in Israel. The inconclusive outcome of the war probably contributed to the strengthening of the right wing in the February 2009 elections—as did the generally unsatisfactory outcome of the Gaza disengagement. It appears that neither a dovish policy of evacuation and dismantling of settlements nor a military onslaught on Hamas has succeeded in granting Israel what it looked for on the Gaza border: a modicum of peace and quiet.

In the biblical story, Samson, provoked by the Philistines, symbolically carried away the gates of Gaza on his shoulders. Like Samson, Israel today is strong but vulnerable; and the gates of Gaza may be too heavy for it, whether it controls Gaza or leaves it.

GETTING IN / GETTING OUT

8

9/11 and the Road to Iraq

NICOLAUS MILLS

SINCE 2004, accounts of how the Bush administration maneuvered the United States into a war of choice in Iraq with the false claim that Saddam Hussein possessed weapons of mass destruction have quickly made it onto the best-seller list. It is easy to see why. At the height of their power, Bush and his advisors often seemed indifferent to the charge that they had invaded Iraq without hard evidence of Saddam's military capability. Paul Wolfowitz, Donald Rumsfeld's deputy defense secretary, told the press in 2003, "The truth is that for reasons that have a lot to do with the U.S. government bureaucracy, we settled on the one issue that everyone could agree on, which was weapons for mass destruction as the core reason."

Today, the trouble with these accounts of the Bush administration's approach to the Iraq War is that they provide too narrow a picture of America in the wake of 9/11. They fail to show how in the eighteen-month run-up to the Iraq War between September 11, 2001, and the start of combat operations on March 20, 2003, the

United States developed a 9/11 culture that made war seem like a logical next step in preventing another terrorist attack.

To say this is not to exempt the Bush administration from the charge that it was so determined to go to war with Iraq that it was willing to use dubious intelligence—or simply cherry-pick the facts—in order to justify invasion. But it is to argue that blame for the Iraq War cannot simply be pinned on the deceptions of the Bush administration, serious as these deceptions were. Such an analysis is too easy on the rest of us. It ignores the widespread anger that early on led the *New York Post* to print a column calling on the president to "kill the bastards" responsible for 9/11 and "if Saddam Hussein makes so much as a peep, do him, too." The 9/11 culture that emerged in the wake of the attacks on the World Trade Center and Pentagon owed much to the Bush administration's maneuverings, but by 2002, that culture had taken on a life of its own that made what the Bush administration did openly even more important than what it did covertly.

America the Vulnerable

In a 2004 essay, "Addicted to 9/11," *New York Times* columnist Thomas Friedman declared, "I want a president who can one day restore Sept. 11 to its rightful place on the calendar: as the day after Sept. 10 and before Sept. 12. I do not want it to become a day that defines us. . . . We're about the Fourth of July." Friedman's resentment of the way in which 9/11 has been inflated certainly makes sense, but at the same time, he is far too dismissive of the reasons why 9/11 quickly went from being a terrible event to a state of mind.

The attacks on the World Trade Center and the Pentagon shocked the country in a way that went far beyond the immediate loss of life and property they caused. The World Trade Center had been attacked once before. On February 26, 1993, Ramzi Yousef, the son of a Palestinian mother and a Pakistani father, who had grown up in Kuwait, parked a truck filled with a massive homemade bomb inside the World Trade Center garage, causing an explosion that blew through six stories of steel and cement, leaving six dead and 1,042 injured in its wake. But the 9/11 attacks were so different in their quality and careful planning from the 1993 attack that they transformed American thinking by puncturing—in a way that has not been repaired—the belief that the United States was a safe haven compared to the rest of the world. The deadliness of the 9/11 attacks made it reasonable for Americans to conclude that terrorists willing to use passenger planes as weapons against civilians would not hesitate to employ weapons of mass destruction if they could get their hands on them.

"We are all American," Jean-Marie Colombani, editor of *Le Monde*, observed on September 12, 2001, in a front-page editorial that was at once an expression of sympathy and a recognition of the blow 9/11 dealt American exceptionalism. The sense of security that even the Second World War had barely dented was over in a matter of hours, and in its place was an unprecedented set of fears about the steps America needed to take to defend itself. As Democratic senator Christopher Dodd and Republican senator Chuck Hagel wrote in a joint *New York Times* op-ed in the fall of 2001, "The events of Sept. 11 shattered any illusion that America is secure from foreign attack." Americans shared this dark view. In October 2001, 85 percent, according to the Gallup poll, believed that a future terrorist attack was likely, and a year later, 60 percent still believed a future terrorist attack was likely.

In both the Second World War and the Cold War, Americans were certain who their enemies were and how to deal with them. Their enemies were other nation-states that could be defeated or, at a minimum, neutralized by America's military superiority. The danger of atomic annihilation during the Cold War years proved scary, but the threat of mutually assured destruction brought with it a hope that the average American found reassuring. As long as the Soviet Union and the United States did not have a death wish, they had a basis for settling their disputes without direct nuclear confrontation.

But 9/11, Americans understood, changed this uneasy historical arrangement. The terrorists who caused 9/11 were not part of another nation-state. They were men bound by no set of conventional rules about waging war. Provided they were willing to die—whether for ideological reasons or because they believed a martyr's death was a prelude to paradise—there was no obvious counterthreat that America could rely on to deter them. On September 11, a fourth hijacked plane, United Flight 93, was brought down in Shanksville, Pennsylvania, before it could reach its intended target in Washington, D.C. The passengers of Flight 93, aware from their cell phones that two terrorist-flown planes had already crashed into the World Trade Center, saved countless lives by their decision to fight back, but in the wake of 9/11, Americans would always be waiting for the next fourth plane.

The events of 9/11 showed that preparations for a terrorist attack, unlike one by a traditional army, did not depend on a large buildup of men and materiel, and, by the same token, defeat did not pose the kinds of problems it did for conventional military leaders. A terrorist group could be stopped a dozen times, a hundred times. It did not matter, so long as the group had enough recruits to draw on for the future. The terrorists who targeted America on 9/11 knew their deaths were a certainty whether they succeeded or failed in their mission. They were not hoping to beat the odds, and in the kind of asymmetric warfare they waged, they did not worry about a string of setbacks. If just once in a while they broke through America's defenses, they made their point: the military might of the United States could not protect it from a small, determined group willing to die.

From this sense of American vulnerability, a unique 9/11 culture began to emerge. When the attack on Pearl Harbor—the day with which 9/11 is most often compared—occurred, America's angry response was unambiguous; the Second World War culture that evolved after December 7, 1941, helped bring about a united country. From armed forces in which 16.4 million Americans served to Victory Gardens that at their peak accounted for 40 percent of all the vegetables grown in the United States, Americans devoted more and more of their energies to defeating Japan and Germany. By contrast, 9/11 culture never had that kind of unifying hold on America. September 11 was not followed by a military draft, a dramatic increase in taxes, or a presidential appeal for sacrifice.

When we look at how 9/11 affected the United States, we see a response based, on the one hand, on widely shared fears and, on the other hand, on the belief that the Cold War doctrine of containment that George Kennan had put forward in 1947 for dealing with the Soviet Union's expansion was outmoded. But it was not just the Cold War era that 9/11 made irrelevant. It also made irrelevant the unipolar dominance in world affairs that America enjoyed during the twelve years between the fall of the Berlin Wall in 1989 and the fall of the World Trade Center in 2001. On 9/11, the post–Cold War era—along with the assumption that for the foreseeable future America was going to reign as the world's lone superpower in an era free from major conflict—ended as dramatically as it began. The humanitarian challenges the country had faced during the Clinton years, in Somalia, in the former Yugoslavia, and in Rwanda gave way to concerns in which Americans now asked, Are we doing enough to protect ourselves?

Images of Disaster

The speed with which 9/11 culture fostered a new cult of masculinity was captured by conservative critic Peggy Noonan in an October 12, 2001, *Wall Street Journal* op-ed, "Welcome Back, Duke," in which she observed, "From the ashes of September 11 arise the manly virtues." But especially in the eighteen months between 9/11 and the start of the Iraq War, what made 9/11 culture so powerful was that it became pervasive, influencing everything from pop music and architecture to daily politics.

The 2001 events that had made headlines prior to 9/11—from Bush's rejection of the Kyoto Protocol on global warming to Barry Bonds's pursuit of the single-season home-run record—quickly came to seem part of a distant era. Overnight, Americans found that the pictures they carried in their heads of 9/11 shaped their sense of how they were prepared to deal with its causes, and that their view of the causes of 9/11 in turn led them to decide on the steps starting over required both by way of mourning the victims and by way of preventing a second 9/11 from happening.

The images of 9/11 that Americans began using in 2001 to define the attack immediately set the tone for all that followed. For historic comparison, we need only look at the front page of the *New York Times* for December 8, 1941. There, just below the headline, "Japan Wars on U.S. and Britain," we see a map of where the fighting in the Pacific is going on. But neither on December 8, nor the next day, nor the day after that did the *Times* carry pictures of the American fleet burning in Pearl Harbor. Pictures of the actual attack did not reach America until December 14, when Secretary of the Navy Frank Knox brought them with him on his flight from Oahu, and they were not released to the *Times* and other papers until December 16, twenty-four hours after Knox reported to the nation on Pearl Harbor. The opposite pattern was true for the events of 9/11, which millions of Americans witnessed on their television sets in real time. Beneath the *Times*'s September 12, 2001, banner headline, "U.S. Attacked," there were multiple pictures of the burning towers, and on page 7 the *Times* carried the picture that became the most horrifying of all to Americans—a telephoto shot of a man unable to escape from the World Trade Center falling to his death, choosing to jump rather than burn.

Richard Drew, the photographer of the 9/11 "falling man" picture, first won fame for himself in 1968 with the grim photos that he took of Robert Kennedy after he was killed by Sirhan Sirhan at the Ambassador Hotel in Los Angeles. But Drew's 2001 falling man photograph, which was shown around the world, caused such anger among American newspaper readers—who saw it as exploitative—that it was shunned by most U.S. editors after September 12. The falling man photograph did not need, however, to be endlessly reproduced for its impact to be felt throughout the country. Within days, two sets of 9/11 images had become an indelible part of American life. The first set focused on the victims of the World Trade Center and Pentagon attacks whose lives were taken from them without warning. The second set focused on the 9/11 rescuers, epitomized in the public's mind by Thomas Franklin's *Bergen Record* picture of three firefighters raising a flag over the World Trade Center's smoking ruins in a pose reminiscent of the marines in Joe Rosenthal's iconic Iwo Jima photograph from the Second World War.

The Drew-Franklin photos, like the thousands of amateur photographs of missing loved ones that appeared on buildings and makeshift memorials throughout New York City, were complementary in the combination of grief and pride they evoked, but they also provided an early indication of how little self-criticism America was prepared to tolerate in the wake of 9/11. When televangelist Jerry Falwell, appearing on the Reverend Pat Robertson's Christian Broadcasting Network's *700 Club*, declared that the "secular and anti-Christian environment" of the United States was behind God's decision to "allow the enemies of America to give us what we probably deserve," he unleashed a backlash that quickly forced him to apologize for saying that 9/11 reflected God's judgment.

The media were especially tough on those who claimed that America was asking for it. From October 2001 to November 2002, the *New Republic* ran an "Idiocy Watch" column that regularly satirized anyone who suggested America bore responsibility for 9/11. At the same time, a series of influential writers on the left also went out of their way to disassociate themselves from the idea that America got what it deserved on 9/11 or that it was "a leading terrorist state," as MIT's Noam Chomsky argued. "The terrorism that burst upon us this September cannot be understood, solely or even preponderantly, as a reaction to U.S. global or Middle Eastern policy," *American Prospect* editor Harold Meyerson cautioned in the magazine's October 2001 issue." And in the January–February 2002 issue of *Mother Jones*, in an essay ironically titled "Blaming America First," Todd Gitlin challenged the thinking of the country's "left-wing fundamentalists" who saw the attacks of 9/11 "as nothing more than an outgrowth of U.S. policy."

Starting Over

By contrast, what Americans and the mainstream media did have an appetite for was investigative reporting that showed America's intelligence agencies had not been diligent enough in responding to the information they already had about terrorists. The best early reporting on this subject was an 8,500-word January 14, 2002, *New Yorker* article, "The Counter-Terrorist," by Lawrence Wright, who later received the Pulitzer Prize for his book *The Looming Tower: Al-Qaeda and the Road to 9/11*. The hero of Wright's article was John O'Neill, a former FBI agent who had left the bureau because he found that his warnings to his superiors about Al Qaeda were never treated with the seriousness he believed they required. Wright was far from alone in doing the kind of investigative journalism that faulted the FBI and the CIA for sloppy intelligence work. The same fault finding was central to *Time*'s "How the FBI Blew the Case," *Newsweek*'s "What Went Wrong," the *Wall Street Journal*'s "FAA Chose Not to Warn Airlines on Pivotal Arrest Before Sept. 11," and the *New York Times*'s "F.B.I. Chief Admits 9/11 Might Have Been Detectable."

This kind of investigative journalism was welcome because it paved the way for starting over. If prior to 9/11 the country had been too soft and too slow in responding to terrorist threats, there was now justification for reversing course. On September 20, just nine days after the attacks on the World Trade Center and the Pentagon, Bush responded to the country's anxiety by creating an Office of Homeland Security, and on October 8 his choice to head that office, former Pennsylvania governor Tom Ridge, officially took charge with widespread approval.

At Ridge's and the Bush administration's disposal was $40 billion in emergency spending that Congress had approved with little debate. Not until November 22, 2002, did the Office of Homeland Security become the cabinet level Department of Homeland Security, but in the intervening months the president had virtual carte blanche to do as he wanted in matters of domestic security and in dealing with an anthrax scare initially feared to be the work of Al Qaeda.

The Democrats were not about to stand in his way. When the now-controversial USA Patriot Act came up for a vote in October, the president had no trouble getting approval of provisions that allowed the government to detain immigrants without charges and lowered the legal standards for intelligence wiretaps. The House passed the Patriot Act on October 24 by an overwhelming 356-66 margin, and a day later in the Senate, the only no vote came from Wisconsin's liberal Democrat Russ Feingold.

Most Americans found it only natural that they should be on the lookout for new terrorist threats. In the fall of 2001, the instant popularity of *24*, a Fox television show in which Jack Bauer, a dedicated

CIA counterterrorism expert played by Kiefer Sutherland, does not hesitate to use torture to stop America's enemies, reflected the country's desire to be made safe again and its willingness to pay a high price for security.

Even more change was on the way. Security checks at airport terminals and a color-coded Homeland Security Assessment System quickly became routine in America, visible reminders of how dangerous ordinary life had become, and in New York City the safety measures were even more extreme, with the increased use of surveillance cameras in Lower Manhattan and the police department's creation of an intelligence unit staffed by analysts speaking, among other languages, Urdu, Pashto, Farsi, and Hindi.

During this same period, a fortified Washington, D.C., marked by the proliferation of bollards around public buildings and national monuments, came to epitomize 9/11's architectural impact. In 1998, an underground Capitol Visitor Center was approved by Congress after a gunman killed two Capitol police officers while they were on duty, and in that same year, following bombings of the U.S. embassies in Kenya and Tanzania, Jersey barriers were installed around the Washington Monument. But in the wake of 9/11, plans for making Washington safe from terrorists escalated.

At Metro subway stations, the changes were subtle; 1,140 trash receptacles were removed and replaced with 400 bomb-resistant trash containers. But elsewhere the changes were highly visible. The Capitol Visitor Center, an underground complex that took up 580,000 square feet and cost $621 million—more than double the planned amount—grew exponentially with the addition of tunnels designed to serve as evacuation routes, and by early 2003 the National Park Service plans for increasing security at the Washington Monument included a defensive perimeter of stone walls as well as the requirement (later cancelled following criticism from the Commission of Fine Arts and preservationists) that visitors enter the monument via a 400-foot entry tunnel from a lodge on the east side of the monument grounds.

Making Victims Whole

For the country, taking precautions was only part of starting over in the wake of 9/11. Equally important, as far as most Americans were concerned, was doing as much as possible for the 9/11 victims and their families. So often American culture has been about forgetting the past and concentrating on the future, but at the core of 9/11 culture—making it readily convertible into a war culture—was the idea of preserving both the grief and grievances that came with 9/11.

The first step in trying to help the 9/11 victims came in trying to make the families of those who died financially whole. The 9/11 widows who had been pregnant at the time of the attacks were a special concern, and the private charity efforts on behalf of the widows, who would later be described as "perfect virgins of grief," peaked on the first anniversary of 9/11 at a much-publicized gathering sponsored by the Independent Women's Forum. One hundred and two 9/11 widows and their post-9/11 children were flown to New York by the forum for a baby shower and luncheon at Cipriani, a posh Manhattan restaurant, where on taking her seat each widow found a toy angel and a $4,000 check waiting for her.

But the most important effort to help the 9/11 families get back on their feet was not private. It was government sponsored. On September 21, 2001, Congress passed the Air Transportation Safety and System Stabilization Act with one eye on bailing out the now-troubled airlines and the other eye on helping the victims of 9/11 with an open-ended, federal Victim Compensation Fund. Kenneth R. Feinberg, a Washington mediator best known for his part in resolving an Agent Orange class action suit dating back to the Vietnam

War, was appointed special master of the 9/11 fund, and by late December he had set out the rules for compensating the families of the 9/11 victims. They included a $250,000 award for pain and suffering and an additional $50,000 for each dependent, a figure that by March 2002 was changed to $100,000, with the result that the average award—before any mandated deductions for life insurance, pensions, and government benefits—climbed from $1.65 million to $1.85 million.

The country was not, however, satisfied with just helping the families of the 9/11 victims return to normal lives. Americans were also determined to make sure that those who died on 9/11 were remembered. There was a National Day of Prayer and Remembrance on the Friday following 9/11, and by the next week the media began stressing the trauma experienced by the 9/11 survivors in a series of television programs and newspaper articles that centered on how those who had lost a family member were coping with their lives. On September 18, 2001, Diane Sawyer led the way on *Good Morning America* with a show that featured two United Flight 93 widows. Two months later, the Gannett News Service published "For Families of Victims, No Holiday from the Pain of 9/11." In 2002, the news stories and programs devoted to 9/11 families increased exponentially. Montel Williams did a program on the "Fiancées and Wives Left Behind." Katie Couric devoted a nightly news feature to the "Wives and Mothers of Victims of Flight 93." Barbara Walters did a special on "Families Left Behind." The national appetite for such looks back in time was, it turned out, unlimited. The most important and visible effort at memorializing the men and women who died on 9/11 came with the reconstruction of the massive World Trade Center site in New York. Early on, the city's mayor, Rudolph Giuliani, set the tone for the terms under which the reconstruction would be discussed when he declared, "If it were up to me, I'd devote the entire sixteen acres to the memorial." Especially in New York City, ordinary citizens quickly became involved in the plans for the site, showing up in record numbers in 2002 at design hearings and making it clear that they did not want a rebuilt World Trade Center in which real estate interests were paramount. The result was that in February 2003 Daniel Libeskind, a Bronx-born architect whose best-known building before 2003 was the Jewish Museum in Berlin, was chosen to be the master planner for the World Trade Center.

Distinguishing Libeskind's plans from those of his better-known architectural rivals was his insistence on emphasizing the tragedy of 9/11 in a way that captured the sentiments of the public and the 9/11 families. In addition to a skyscraper designed to reach to the symbolic height of 1,776 feet, Libeskind's Ground Zero plans featured a memorial area thirty feet below grade that left part of the original World Trade Center slurry wall exposed and a Wedge of Light triangle, designed to let the sun shine between the surrounding buildings on each September 11 for the exact time and duration of the 9/11 attack.

The Politics of Preemption

The selection committee that a month before the start of the Iraq War named Libeskind master planner was certainly not motivated by the idea of providing aid and comfort to the Bush administration. But the architectural thinking about the meaning of 9/11 that vaulted Libeskind into the role of master planner for the World Trade Center paralleled the thinking that had led Congress in the fall of 2002 to give the president the power he wanted to go to war on his terms. In both cases, grief and fear were the dominant forces.

With Libeskind, grief and fear supported architecture that, above all else, paid homage to the tragedy of 9/11. With Congress, on the other hand, grief and fear supported approving whatever steps the president thought were required to protect America. By, 2002 no politician had put himself in a position to benefit more from the rise of 9/11 culture and the surge of patriotism accompanying it than George W. Bush. In January 2002, Karl Rove, Bush's chief political adviser, spoke openly of making the president's handling of the war on terror the focus of the 2002 midterm election. "We can go to the country on this issue because they trust the Republican Party to do a better job of protecting and strengthening America's military might and thereby protecting America," Rove observed in a widely reported speech before the Republican National Committee.

Rove's strategy was a perfect fit for the president. In the days immediately following 9/11, Bush had faltered. He spent most of 9/11 being shuttled from hiding place to hiding place by the Secret Service, and when he finally addressed the nation on the night of the attacks, he was far from inspiring. By comparison to New York's Giuliani, who rushed to the World Trade Center site to take personal command of operations and soon appeared on television assuring New Yorkers that they had no need to panic, the president seemed indecisive. "Our President Shows He's No Giuliani," a *Newsday* headline proclaimed.

But the president recovered quickly from his early missteps. At a meeting with the rescue workers at Ground Zero on Friday, September 14, he made headlines with an impromptu speech declaring, "I hear you. The rest of the world hears you, and the people who knocked down these buildings will hear all of us soon." From this point on, the president was able to govern from a position of strength and, despite his economic policies, identify himself with the working-class heroes of Ground Zero. The image of the president standing on the rubble of the Twin Towers with his arm around a New York firefighter, talking through a bullhorn, would make a lasting impression on voters.

From the start, Bush had labeled the 9/11 attacks "mass murder" committed by faceless cowards, and the anxieties that shaped the public's initial response to 9/11 reinforced his views. Americans did not want to see their president fail in a crisis, and in the aftermath of 9/11, voters were more than willing to cut him slack on those occasions when he did not perform up to par. From a low of 51 percent in the last Gallup poll taken before September 11, his approval rating shot up to 90 percent in Gallup's September 21–22 poll, then hovered between 86 percent and 89 percent for the rest of the year.

By the fall of 2002, the president was ready to carry out Rove's midterm election strategy and take advantage of the political culture 9/11 had fostered. Bush's first step in 2002 came on September 17, when he issued the "National Security Strategy of the United States," which brought together ideas that he had been voicing since the fall of 2001, when he promised to undertake "a lengthy campaign" to bring about "the defeat of the global terror network." At the core of the papers and speeches that made up the "National Security Strategy" was the idea that the Cold War doctrine of containment was over. The United States, as the president had declared in his June 1, 2002, graduation speech at West Point, could no longer rely on conventional military deterrence and support from its allies to defend itself. In the new age of terrorism, it was crucial, he argued, for America to identify and destroy any threat "before it reaches our borders." America now reserved for itself the right of "acting preemptively."

The danger of such a doctrine was the combination of unilateral power that it gave to America and the risks it posed if other nations claimed such power for themselves. But in the fall of 2002, most Americans did not worry about that. Voters were comforted by the idea that the president had devised a foreign policy doctrine that put America first, no matter what other nations did. In September, 71 percent of those surveyed in a Gallup poll said that the government's actions had prevented further terrorist attacks. Bush was as a result strongly positioned to build the 2002 Republican political campaign around the idea that he needed more members of his party in Congress to help him carry out the policies that would protect America from future terrorist attacks.

Democrats, already on record supporting the president on the war in Afghanistan, which a Gallup poll showed had a public approval rating of 91 percent in March 2002 and 83 percent six months later in September, found themselves in a no-win situation. They had no grounds for complaining about the president's pursuit of the Afghanistan War, and when they tried to switch the focus of the election to the economy, they got little traction with security-conscious voters.

Bush, however, was still not through taking advantage of the 9/11 political climate. His next step was to ask for a resolution giving him authority in advance to use force in Iraq if Saddam Hussein did not fully comply with United Nations inspectors searching his country for weapons of mass destruction. The force resolution was a bold bid by the president for unchecked power, and the counter-response of Senate Democrats and moderate Republicans was a bill by Democratic Senator Joe Biden and Republican Senator Richard Lugar of the Senate Foreign Relations Committee requiring the president to get a UN Security Council resolution for war or make a determination that the weapons Iraq possessed constituted "so grave" a threat to the United States that war was necessary.

In practice, the Biden-Lugar resolution would not have constrained Bush for long, but he still found it onerous, and once again he got what he wanted when he asked for more power to protect the country. On October 11, the president won bipartisan congressional approval to use military force against Iraq as long as such force was "consistent" with America's ongoing efforts to fight terrorism. The vote in the House was 296 to 133, and in the Senate it was 77 to 23, with liberal Democrats doing little to fight the president when he declared, "I don't want to get a resolution which ties my hands."

In a speech on the Senate floor, liberal Democrat Jay Rockefeller of West Virginia, a member of the Senate Intelligence Committee, backed the president, insisting that Saddam's current weapons "pose a very real threat to the United States," and among the force resolution's final supporters were Democratic House minority leader Richard Gephardt and Democratic senators Tom Daschle, Harry Reid, Hillary Clinton, and John Kerry, who in casting his vote declared, "I will vote yes because I believe it is the best way to hold Saddam Hussein accountable. . . . It means America speaks with one voice."

If the vote had been held after the November elections, Senator Ted Kennedy speculated, there would have been more opposition to the force resolution, but for liberal and moderate Democrats alike, much closer to the truth was military historian Andrew Bacevich's observation that "opposition to war had become something of a third rail: only the very brave or the very foolhardy dared to venture anywhere near it." Democrats remembered that in 1991 their opposition to the Gulf War had made them seem weak on national security issues, and for the most part they made passage of the force resolution as uncontroversial as they could. At key moments in the debate over the resolution, as few as ten of the Senate's one hundred senators were on the floor, prompting the *Washington Post*'s Dana Milbank to report, "America took a step closer to war yesterday— with a yawn."

Playing the Fear Card

With passage of the force resolution, the likelihood of war with Iraq became greater than at any time since September 11, and the willingness of the country to go to war at this time was increased by a series of reports from Judith Miller in the *New York Times* about Iraq's weapons of mass destruction and its quest for atomic bomb materials. Miller, who had been with the *Times* since 1977, won a

Pulitzer Prize in 2001, and served in the Middle East as the *Times*'s Cairo bureau chief, was a highly respected reporter, known for her exclusives, and in the fall of 2002 the accounts she published about the dangers Iraq posed had an enormous impact on the debate over whether America should go to war.

The article that received the most attention was one Miller coauthored with Michael Gordon, the *Times* senior military correspondent. "U.S. Says Hussein Intensifies Quest for A-Bomb Parts" appeared on page one of the Sunday, September 8, 2002, edition and in chilling language warned, "Iraq has stepped up its quest for nuclear weapons and has embarked on a worldwide hunt for materials to make an atomic bomb." In the past the *Times* had been highly critical of Bush's foreign policy, and so the reports by Miller (she left the paper in 2005 after a bitter, public controversy about the inaccuracy of her reporting and her over-reliance on information from Iraqi dissidents) gave the president new credibility. A worst-case scenario based on unverified intelligence estimates began to take on a life of its own.

In addition to a united Republican Party (Lincoln Chafee of Rhode Island was the only Republican senator to vote against the force resolution), President Bush now had a newly energized conservative right behind him. During the 1990s, the conservative right had opposed nation-building in Africa as well as in the former Yugoslavia on the grounds that such humanitarian efforts were not in America's self-interest. But in the wake of 9/11, conservatives began to call for a militant reengagement with the world that made force a first alternative. In his September 28, 2001, *Washington Post* column, Charles Krauthammer called on America to go after Syria, Iraq, and Iran as soon as it took care of the Taliban in Afghanistan, and in the right-wing *Weekly Standard* Robert Kagan and William Kristol insisted, "For the war on terrorism to succeed, Saddam Hussein must be removed." In battling terrorism, those on the right believed, the United States was really fighting World War IV.

The World War IV idea was initially put forward in the *Wall Street Journal* in November 2001 by Eliot A. Cohen, who later took a leave from the School of Advanced International Studies at Johns Hopkins to accept a position in the Bush State Department. The idea was expanded on in *Commentary* in February 2002 by Norman Podhoretz, the magazine's editor from 1960 to 1995. Cohen and Podhoretz argued from the same premise: like the Cold War (World War III in their thinking), World War IV was bound to be a long war in which America should not hesitate to take advantage of its military superiority if it wanted to avoid more trouble in the future.

In the fall of 2002, Bush was, however, still not in a position to do as he pleased. Although 9/11 culture had helped move the country to the brink of war, an Iraq war was still not inevitable at this point. Polls showed that slightly more than half of all Americans favored sending ground troops into Iraq to remove Saddam Hussein, but this pro-war sentiment was qualified. Americans were divided on whether the Bush administration had gone far enough with its diplomatic efforts in dealing with Iraq. In a *New York Times*/CBS News poll published in February 2003, 66 percent of Americans said they approved of the United States taking military action against Iraq to remove Saddam Hussein from power, but 59 percent also said that they believed the United States should give the UN weapons inspectors more time to do their work, and 63 percent said the United States should not act without the support of its allies.

Even more important for Bush, there was skepticism within the foreign policy establishment about a war of choice with Iraq. In August 2002, Brent Scowcroft, national security adviser under presidents Gerald Ford and George H. W. Bush, dealt the administration an unexpected setback when on CBS's *Face the Nation* he warned against a U.S. invasion of Iraq. Then just over a week later, in a widely quoted *Wall Street Journal* op-ed piece, Scowcroft argued that beginning a war in Iraq without broad international support "put at risk our campaign against terrorism as well as stability and security in a vital region of the world."

Flight of the Liberal Hawks

As the country moved closer to war, Scowcroft never changed the position that he took in his "Don't Attack Saddam" *Wall Street Journal* op-ed. It was a different story for the liberal left. In the run-up to the Iraq War, the intellectuals of the liberal left were of two minds. Those such as Robert Kuttner of the *American Prospect* and the editors of the *Nation* were outspoken opponents of an Iraq war, believing that a preemptive attack set a dangerous precedent in international law. But opposing them was a powerful group of liberal internationalists who, to varying degrees, favored war as the only way to overthrow Saddam Hussein.

The most dramatic moment for the liberal internationalists came shortly after the 2002 midterm elections. At a November 22 forum at New York University entitled "Ambiguities of Intervention: Iraq and After," a distinguished panel of liberal thinkers gathered to discuss a possible war with Iraq. The panel included former UN undersecretary general Sir Brian Urquhart, former Iranian ambassador to the UN Mansour Farhang, historian Frances FitzGerald, culture critic Todd Gitlin, political philosopher Michael Walzer, and Iraqi dissident Kanan Makiya. All on the panel, save Makiya, were filled with doubts about or opposed an American-led war in Iraq. But in the end, Makiya, the last speaker of the evening, was the one who drew the greatest cheers from the NYU audience when he argued that war presented the only chance for removing Saddam Hussein from power and achieving democracy in Iraq. "I rest my moral case on the following," Makiya declared. "If there's a sliver of a chance of it happening, a 5 to 10 percent chance, you have a moral obligation, I say, to do it."

Makiya's motives in calling for an invasion of Iraq could not have been farther from those of the Bush administration. He was not worried about the threat Saddam posed to the West. He was worried about the brutal tyranny Saddam exercised over his own country. The problem was that in the context of post-9/11 America, Makiya's call for invasion had the effect of strengthening the administration's hand. His moral obligation argument simply provided the administration with another reason for going to war.

The same linkage with the Bush administration also held true for a group of liberal thinkers and writers who came to be known as "liberal hawks" because of their belief that Saddam Hussein needed to be overthrown. The impact of this small but influential group on the Iraq debate was captured in February 2003 in a widely read *New York Times* op-ed piece, "The I-Can't-Believe-I'm-a-Hawk Club," by Bill Keller, the *Times*'s future executive editor. "Thanks to all these grudging allies, Mr. Bush will be able to claim, with justification, that the coming war is a far cry from the rash, unilateral adventure some of his advisers would have settled for," Keller wrote.

Keller's prediction proved accurate. Over the course of the 1990s, the liberal hawks, among them George Packer of the *New Yorker*; Jacob Weisberg of *Slate*; Paul Berman, author of *Terror and Liberalism*; Michael Ignatieff, director of the Carr Center for Human Rights Policy at Harvard's Kennedy School of Government; and Kenneth Pollack, a member of the National Security Council during the Clinton administration, had become liberal interventionists. Believing that America should have done more to stop the ethnic cleansing and genocide in the former Yugoslavia and Rwanda, they called for a new American engagement in world affairs that put an end to the cautious retreats of the post–Vietnam era.

As Packer observed just months before the Iraq War began, Bosnia "turned these liberals into hawks." In their writing the liberal hawks themselves spoke openly about how the humanitarian crises of the past, particularly those of the nineties, had affected them and made their fear of more mass killings in Iraq central to their belief in an invasion. In justifying his initial support of the Iraq War ("I came down on the pro-war side by a whisker" was the way he explained his decision), Packer cited "the legacy of the Halabja poison gas attack" that Saddam had unleashed in 1988 against Iraq's Kurdish population. Weisberg made the same point, calling Saddam "a genocidal butcher on an epic scale." For Berman, Saddam's Iraq was a land of "mass graves" with "a population crushed by thirty-five years of Baathist boots stomping on their faces." For Ignatieff, the justification for war was Halabja and the "malignancy" of Saddam's future intentions, and for Pollack, Saddam's "murderous regime" with its violations of "every moral code in existence" was grounds for U.S. action

Worried that, as Bill Keller had predicted, his stance, along with that of the other liberal hawks, would help the Bush administration, Ignatieff complained, "I don't like the company I am keeping, but I think they are right on the issue." It was a principled stance for Ignatieff and the other liberal hawks to take, but as the Bush administration continued to press for war, it was also a stance that prevented liberals from mounting effective and unified opposition to the president. The liberal hawks were in no position to challenge the president and at the same time call, as Paul Berman did, for taking "a harder line that might bring about Saddam's collapse peacefully or, if need be, not peacefully."

In the end, the nuanced Iraq War that the liberal hawks wanted was not the war for which 9/11 culture had paved the way, but that distinction ceased to matter by February 2003, when the secretary of state, Colin Powell, with George Tenet, director of the Central Intelligence Agency sitting directly behind him, went before the UN General Assembly to announce that America had "deeply troubling" evidence that Iraq possessed weapons of mass destruction.

War was war as far as most Americans were concerned, and in the weeks following Powell's speech there was no stirring up the kind of antiwar opposition that might have been possible if passage of the force resolution in the fall of 2002 had generated significant controversy. Americans were not deterred by army chief of staff Eric Shinseki's warning, made in testimony before the Senate Armed Services Committee, that several hundred thousand troops, more than double the administration's calculation, would be needed to occupy Iraq; nor were they fazed by Defense Department undersecretary Douglas Feith's admission, made at Senate Foreign Relations Committee hearings, that there were "enormous uncertainties" surrounding the administration's war plans.

From the public's point of view, Powell's speech, which drew widespread support in the media, was never significantly challenged by the left or by the massive antiwar demonstrations of 2002 and 2003, which in their "No Sanctions, No Bombing" slogans all but ignored the question of how to stop Saddam from committing more crimes against his own population. The liberal hawks, who later became strong critics of the conduct of the Iraq War, had managed to put themselves in a situation in which their differences with the Bush administration seemed minimal just when 9/11 culture gave the president a level of power he would never again enjoy. From here on in, there was no slowing the move toward war.

9

The Persistence of Empire

DAVID BROMWICH

THE resolution required to get out of an imperial or a humanitarian-improvement occupation is not different in kind from the heave of the will required for getting in. The problem is that getting in was made possible by a morale of entitlement that speaks the language of self-sacrifice and decency; this one-way bridge of excuses is still in place when the moment comes for getting out. If the choice to invade and occupy were actually derived from conscience, our duties might be revised once the mission was shown to be riddled with atrocities. Yet the occupying power will always be hampered by the emotion of conviction that drove it to attack in the first place.

A different bridge of excuses has sometimes proved serviceable. The majority of the people in the occupied country can be portrayed, often with a degree of truth, as victims of an active and energetic faction. The mission then comes to be seen as a salvage operation on behalf of the nonpolitical or the less political, the patient and long-suffering who mean no harm but are in danger of being engrossed by the appetites of dangerous and violent men. Violence, of course, is the method of the invading as of the insurgent army. But in the minds of imperial leaders, imperial wars are fought in some measure for the sake of passive sufferers, who will find their freedom as soon as the wicked have been purged—in a year, a decade, or longer.

The public understanding that control of the occupied country is somehow unselfish goes a long way to legitimate staying on. By contrast, empires that actually profess their selfishness are rare. The Belgian interest in the Congo represents an extreme and not an ordinary case; and the hatefulness of such adventurism sets a natural term to its efficacy. Most people, most nations, love themselves more than that. We love the idea that we are good; that we have and practice the best way of life. (The Roman Empire held the latter belief with so unmixed a fervor that its armies could maintain its colonies in subjection without the slightest pang of remorse. The best and luckiest of the colonized might always become Romans.) Self-love feeds on and builds up amour-propre—the sense that we are showing a good face to the world. Hence, imperial conquest naturally mingles high reasons with base motives. For the occupying power, to have gotten in, and to have suffered losses in a foreign place, deepens the tracks of collective self-love to such an extent that no counteraction can be expected from self-reproach.

Only nations that (a) were defeated beyond the ability to pretend otherwise, and (b) had the luck to be well treated by the power that vanquished them may later exemplify the judgments of collective conscience. Germans of the last two generations have been thoughtful about the uses of national power in a way that Americans after Vietnam have not been thoughtful. Indeed, the *Dolchstosslegende* of "how we lost Vietnam" was freely invoked as recently as the 2008 American presidential election. Among the guilty who are only half defeated, the very idea of national conscience is an oxymoron.

The Ideology of Conquest

When conquest and occupation turn into a customary practice for a people not congenitally cruel—and let us agree the English-speaking peoples (as Churchill called us) are not raised to be cruel—the first effects of conquest will be registered in a mood of ecstatic wonder. This mood cannot be coaxed into retraction or reform without an intervening stage of bewilderment caused by setbacks. In British India, after Robert Clive's victory at Plassey in 1757, the transition from imperial triumph to the first glimmers of reform took twenty-five years. In Iraq, violence contracted the necessary span to three or four. This second stage is characterized by doubts that have not yet crystallized into thoughts. The occupying power reflects on itself, with perplexity, as a natural ruler beset by resistance whose motives are unimaginable. (To call the resistance simply evil is to restate in other words this default of imagination.)

It is customary for setbacks to be followed by a new pattern of cruelty—"taking the gloves off"—by the conqueror who now runs prisons and courts while retaining the power to despoil crops and devastate cities. In India in the 1770s, the governor-general of Bengal, Warren Hastings, explained to his superiors that Hindus and Mohammedans alike had been accustomed to a regime of oriental despotism; consequently, the light hand of British commercial rule was inappropriate: their disobedience called for exemplary punishments to drive the lesson home. A parallel system of explanations was deployed by the State Department under Condoleezza Rice. The reconstruction of civil society in Iraq was a harder job than we had envisaged. Why? Because, when the U.S. army rolled in, we discovered that Saddam Hussein, by a design three decades in execution, had destroyed every remnant of the civil society of Iraq, and had infantilized its people to the point where any hope of unassisted self-government was forlorn. There was no civil society there; we had to lift it in. On the other hand, the assassinations of 2003-2005, which robbed Iraq of many hundreds, perhaps thousands, of the teachers, doctors, lawyers, city administrators, and engineers who form the backbone of civil society—these killings (undeterred by U.S. troops) played no part in the official account of Iraq's inward failure. Just so, the depredations of the Rohilla and Maratha wars of the 1770s and early 1780s, paid for or fought by the East India Company, played no part in the British account of the innate corruption and unfitness to rule of Indians of every sect and region. The incidental atrocities of those tribal wars, according to the governor-general, were "justified by the practice of war established among all nations of the East."

Behind the pressure of self-justification there is always a denial of perception, and behind that denial a failure of feeling. When a country has embarked on a foreign war in which self-preservation is a distant and incredible pretext, the ethic of "team spirit" supports the enterprise by infecting a reliable majority in the home country. As the Boer War attests, this spirit touches journalists as surely as lawmakers and soldiers. J. A. Hobson, in *The Psychology of Jingoism*, spoke of the characteristic means by which a war of choice is sold as a war of necessity:

> Dishonesty, in the sense of professing to believe what one does not really believe, is very rare at all times; in this matter it may be safely regarded as undeserving of consideration. Those who profess to believe the war to be just and necessary do honestly believe this. But have they honestly come by this belief? That is the real question. Have they used such reasonable care in unbiased consideration of the evidence as entitles them to claim an honest judgment?. . . The editors of Jingo journals have felt quite safe in continuing to repeat the most audacious falsehoods long after they have been exposed, simply because they knew that their readers, though perfectly aware that journals existed which gave another side, would not look at papers which opposed the war. Now, this attitude of mind has been the rule, and not

the exception, among the classes which boast their education and intelligence, and it is an attitude of dishonesty.

Hobson knew South Africa firsthand, and he knew the interests from Cape Town to London that had pressed for the Boer War. The distinction he mentions, between active dishonesty and "an attitude of dishonesty," applies to the American press and television at every stage of the Iraq War: from the credulous channeling of government evidence to rally popular feeling, to the celebrations of easy triumph, to the baffled nonpolitical coverage of the insurgency, to the ready embrace of "the surge," whose success in a five-month trial was reckoned sufficient to take the war off the front pages of our leading papers for most of 2007 and 2008. A reporter, whether at the State Department or in the streets of Baghdad, may tell "the truth and nothing but the truth" without coming near the whole truth. To recount the good intentions of army officers and not to investigate stories of atrocity involves a habit of self-censorship so commonplace it can pass for mere economy of editing. With the denial of perception and consequent shrinking of sympathy, only our own dead or those of our pledged allies are countable. The others are seen as possibly enemies, and probably hostile in some fashion.

Team spirit introduces another distortion that is harder to grasp because it is universal. People in the home country lose the ability to see the strangeness of their presence in a land several thousand miles away. How difficult it was, and is, for us to look at footage of American soldiers in Vietnam, or at photographs of our soldiers in Iraq, and continue to ask, year after year, "What are we doing there?" The apparatus of opinion, in which heroic stories of sacrifice exert a considerable popular influence, puts the very question out of mind. The strangeness is gradually rendered normal.

We may think we understand the British "Empire in the West" (the American colonies) and the "Empire in the East" (the Indian subcontinent) because there is a received version that commands recognition. The mother country intended a generous partnership with her colonies, but the Americans, embodying "the dissidence of dissent, and the protestantism of the protestant religion," were too heated with radical doctrine to be amenable to normal diplomacy. Whereas with India, the empire found itself in the advance guard of civilization confronting a race in its nonage. As John Robert Seeley wrote in *The Expansion of England* in 1883 (mainly thinking of India), Britain seemed "to have conquered and peopled the world in a fit of absence of mind." Yet the British Empire held a conscious ideology whose traces are legible from Macaulay's "Minute on Education" to Kipling's Barrack-Room Ballads. The American ideology of conquest has left thinner traces; few of those who governed our possessions have had the gift or the ambition to compose an enduring record. Still, there has been a consistent ideology. In the years before the Civil War, Abraham Lincoln remarked the rise of what he called "pro-slavery theology." God had not found a way into Southern justifications of slavery until the 1840s, but as the sectional conflict heated up, theology was called on to supply the answers that convenience and accident had given before. It has been the same, in our own time, with pro-empire geography. Apologists for the Iraq War decided in 2004-2005 that, though the war may have been a mistake, it was not our mistake. Iraq was never meant to be one country. The amalgamation of Shiite and Sunni and Kurdish regions, carved up and combined by the British in the 1920s, had never been built to last. Iraq, it was now discovered, would have been happier if left in three separate parts: this was the burden of an op-ed by Leslie Gelb and Joseph Biden, "Unity Through Autonomy in Iraq," published by the *New York Times* on May 1, 2006. A divided Iraq would make it easier for the autonomous divisions to get along (and perhaps also easier, though Gelb and Biden omitted to say so, for American forces to dominate). This rationalization was also a late discovery of the

British in India, indeed a discovery announced by Seeley: "The truth is that [before the British came] there was no India in the political, and scarcely in any other, sense. The word was a geographical expression, and therefore India was easily conquered, just as Italy and Germany fell an easy prey to Napoleon." Seeley went on to challenge the assumption that "wherever, inside or outside of Europe, there is a country which has a name, there must be a nationality answering to it." Does the lack of a single coherent nationality make a country more proper for conquest or only more susceptible to it? The answer will depend on the extent to which one believes that human status is rightly constituted by national identity.

The most vexing puzzle of pro-empire geography, abetted by pro-nationalist theology, is that in the course of imperial wars the conquering power transforms the people of displaced nations into stateless persons, so that the conquered and displaced now lack precisely the political and legal rights that are more important to human survival than national identity itself.

The justifications of empire never run out. Suppose it is discovered that the conquered nation was actually composed of a number of smaller discrete nations, tribes, or sects. Nonetheless, these smaller units remain a legitimate object for external control and reshaping, since they pose a common problem both for the occupying power and for each other. Radical Islam today is said to present a challenge for the entire world, yet it is also a provocation that the United States has a duty to "engage with" militarily. We are the most militarized country in the world, and "What's the point," as Madeleine Albright said to Colin Powell, "of having this superb military you're always talking about if we can never use it?" So we take the responsibility on behalf of the world for dealing with radical Islam. Yet the casualties we strew in our path are seldom the targets we aim at. Most of the hundreds of thousands killed by the United States thus far in Iraq and Afghanistan were never part of radical Islam;

and the killing contributes to swell the resentment and drive up the hatred to which radical Islam can appeal.

That the United States bears the responsibility for maintaining right over wrong in the world, and that we ought to enforce our sense of responsibility by violence that may permissibly kill hundreds of thousands of the innocent—this doctrine presumes a degree of confidence in ourselves as judges in our own cause that, if we found it in a person, we would recognize as a form of insanity. Yet there are venerable pretexts for so expansive a notion of American altruism. One such pretext was inadvertently given by Lincoln, in a passage of his *Speech on the Dred Scott Decision* that has been admired alike by neoconservative and neoliberal pundits. Lincoln here said of the American founders' use of the words "All men are created equal":

> They meant to set up a standard maxim for free society, which should be familiar to all, and revered by all; constantly looked to, constantly labored for, and even though never perfectly attained, constantly approximated, and thereby constantly spreading and deepening its influence, and augmenting the happiness and value of life to all people of all colors everywhere.

This is a subtle and complex metaphor about the influence of an ideal, and Lincoln meant to evoke a sublime civic achievement rightly admired from afar: a principle to be studied and emulated by a conscious act of the will. "Spreading and deepening" suggests a possibly related idea: a color penetrating a fabric whose extent grows imperceptibly wider. Yet, for the warmest enthusiasts of the expansion of freedom—the sort of lawmaker or journalist to whom Tony Blair could seem "the conscience of the free world"—Lincoln's idea of a principle that "spreads" suggested a more literal way of proceeding. Armies might invade the lands of the oppressed and convey a democratic idealism by force of arms.

It is extremely unlikely that Lincoln had this in mind. In his own time, he was hostile to the idealism of Manifest Destiny. He thought the Mexican War unjust, and made an eloquent speech against it. He also declined the gambit proposed by his secretary of state, William Seward, in March 1861, to work up a national freedom war against Spain and France as a common enterprise to unify the American North and South. On the other hand, it seems possible that the sensibility of Woodrow Wilson vibrated to the call of generous empire that Lincoln's words could seem to present to a latter-day Democrat and Presbyterian elder. And if these particular words were never quoted by George W. Bush—as they were quoted by his father in 1990—the younger Bush paraphrased them often, and with an exalted glow. The idea of an exemplary democracy, which Lincoln intended, is slower to disclose its fruits than the evangelical democracy we have mistaken it for.

When We Can, Not When We Must

It is often said that in the era of globalization the nature of empire has changed. Since commercial and not political domination is what we seek, and since military means are now incidental, America's burdens today are as benign as they are irresistible. Once the world is joined to form a single polite and commercial people, the wars will be over. Yet the co-presence of commercial expansion and war is an older story than we Americans have been trained to recognize. On this point Seeley, because he was an honest defender of empire, makes a convincing antidote to Woodrow Wilson. "The wars of the eighteenth century," he observed, "were incomparably greater and more burdensome than those of the Middle Ages. Those of the seventeenth century were also great. These are precisely the centuries in which England grew more and more a commercial country. England indeed grew ever more warlike at that time as she grew ever more commercial."

America in the late twentieth and early twenty-first centuries has grown more warlike even as we are told that the age of globalization will soon render all wars obsolete. Once again, the resort to war has marched hand in hand with the spread of commerce.

Getting out is made onerous, above all, by the inhibitions of a natural pride. In Vietnam, it took the five years from 1964 to 1968 for even the liberal wing of the Democratic Party to say we ought to include the Vietcong in negotiations; and that war, as Frances FitzGerald recalls, with its adjustments and rising brutality and enhanced dishonesty under President Richard Nixon, went on for another six years. At the end of any such engagement, there remain people in the occupied country who are attached to the occupying power. There remain a larger number, hard to discriminate from the first, who have shown visible loyalty and to whom the occupying power owes a reciprocal debt. These may yet be made into a reason for staying in Iraq, as they were made a reason for staying in Vietnam; the longer we stay, the more of them there are. Yet such loyal followers ought to be cared for as an addition to the duties of leave-taking, and not deployed as a fresh complication to throw doubt on the process. In any case, we cannot judge our actions against a future that is supposed to alter the pattern of the past. Sanely to judge our present state means to place, on one side of the scale, the actual weight of what we have done, and on the other side the things we ought to have done. When the balance of our past action tips far toward injustice, it is well beyond time to be getting out.

"No imperial power," Rajeev Bhargava observes of the British departure from India, "has been known to withdraw from a colony without securing its strategic interests," for the "occupying power," he adds, "must appear, at the very least, to exit on its own terms." This is true of the not wholly defeated, for reasons of national amour-propre. But the words of Lord Chatham to Parliament on the occupation of America are still pertinent: "We shall be forced ultimately to retreat: let us retreat when we can, not when we must." Why, it may finally be asked, is there ever a "must" so long as the occupying power holds command of the field and so long as it can enforce its will as the greater power? An answer memorable in its plainness was given by the North Vietnamese commander General Vo Nguyen Giap. We will defeat the Americans, said Giap, because we cannot leave this country. The Americans will leave because they can.

10

Departing Responsibly

BRENDAN O'LEARY

THE political and military scene in Iraq is best described as a series of truces. All parties await America's exit, and all will try to steer it in their favor. President Barack Obama's moment can be used either to guide Iraq toward a successful federation or to preside over a failed transfer of power, one in which the United States, with bungled intentions, assists divided Arab centralists in Baghdad to go to war with Kurdistan and with each other.

Leaving Iraq with integrity requires the Obama administration to ensure a secure balance of power within Iraq. That is made feasible by Iraq's Constitution, properly understood. It also requires the new administration to encourage clear internal territorial demarcations within Iraq's federation, especially between Kurdistan and al-Iraq al-Arabi. It will have to inhibit fearful or aggrandizing interventions by Iran or Turkey and the provisioning of insurgents by Sunni-Arab dominated states.

These are very tall orders. They can be met. But they will require the administration to be guided by Vice President Joe Biden's federalist instincts and by Secretary of State Hillary Clinton's Kurdish sympathies and not by the centralist dispositions of orthodox Arabists found in the State Department, the Pentagon's planners, and much of Washington's think-tank commentariat.

Numerous foul legacies shape Iraq. Some are partly America's responsibility. They include the Baathists' seizure of power in 1963 and 1968 and, lest we forget, Henry Kissinger's endorsement of the squalid deal between the shah of Iran and Saddam that crushed the fifteen-year Kurdish rebellion of Mustafa Barzani. Expulsions of Kurds, racist Arabization programs, and boundary manipulations followed in Kirkuk and in other "disputed territories," that is, where local Kurdish majorities live amid Arab and other minorities. Ronald Reagan and George H. W. Bush ignored Saddam's genocidal atrocities in 1987 and 1988. They did not want Iran to win the war Saddam had started. Some even tried to blame Tehran for Baghdad's use of chemical weapons against Kurds and Iranians. Later, Kurds and Shiite Arabs were left to flee and fend for themselves after having been called to overthrow Saddam by Bush the elder, who somehow managed to forget he had done so. In the first Gulf War, the "realists"— Brent Scowcroft, James Baker, and Colin Powell—ended the Baathist looting of Kuwait, but decided not to organize the replacement of Saddam's regime. It was presidents from Turkey and France and a British prime minister, aided by Americans with a conscience, who obliged the formation of a safe haven for the Kurds. The Shiite Arabs were not so lucky. The U.S.-sponsored UN sanctions of Iraq followed (1991–2003), driven by Saddam's refusal to comply fully with Security Council orders to destroy weapons-of-mass-destruction programs. The costs were passed to Iraq's children and those outside Saddam's inner circle. Kurdistan's experiment in unofficial autonomy was devastated by triple sanctions—UN on Iraq, Saddam on Kurdistan, and pressure from neighbors that killed its agriculture.

Most observers complete this shameful list with the post-9/11 decision to remove Saddam's regime. Reasonable historians should judge, however, that removing the genocidal Baathists was overdue. The younger Bush made up for his father's mistake, though he did so for the wrong reasons. What was inexcusable was the grotesque mismanagement of regime replacement: the unnecessary and arrogant occupation; the incompetence of American direct rule; the failure to inhibit the disorder that had to follow regime collapse; and the numerous errors of policy and imagination, both well intentioned and malevolent, in the horrors and brutalities that have followed.

This record scarcely inspires confidence, but not all that is malevolent in Iraq is America's responsibility. Moreover, some good has emerged from the Bush administration's intervention, though that is insufficiently recognized.

I refer not to the surge or to the defeat of Al Qaeda in Mesopotamia— which emerged and flourished after the U.S. intervention. The surge is somewhat misunderstood and overrated in importance; the local defeat of Al Qaeda, though entirely welcome, owed most to that organization's eventually self-destructive tactics. I refer instead to Iraq's Constitution, which established its federal government, and to the Kurdistan region—neither made in Washington, though it is sometimes implied otherwise.

The Constitution of 2005 and the successes of the Kurdistan Regional Government (KRG) are the work of Arab and Kurdish politicians and voters. That the Bush administration let these institutions materialize does not mean that they are its creatures or are contaminated by its incompetence. To the contrary, the Constitution and the KRG are what must be protected in making the most honorable of the possible exits.

The responsible transfer of power must be completed with the federal government of Iraq and the Kurdistan Region. These institutions are the expressions of Iraqis' and Kurds' democratic will. Prioritizing their protection provides the right guidelines for the Obama administration to leave Iraq with integrity. The difficulty is that the Arab leadership in Baghdad is at odds with that of the KRG. America will have to back Kurdistan on some key matters and reassure the federal government of their merits. That is the only way a successful transfer of power can be accomplished.

A Feasible Democracy

The British invented modern Iraq by attempting to solder part of historic Kurdistan to al-Iraq al-Arabi. They broke their promise to create an autonomous Kurdistan and invented a deeply dysfunctional and divided polity. A Sunni Arabian Hashemite monarchy, despite intermittent good intentions, reentrenched the Ottoman hierarchy of Sunni over Shia and a new racial and ethnic hierarchy of Arab over Kurd. The consequences were catastrophic, though often unregistered in the West, including in Western scholarship, which mostly read Iraq through the claims of its secularist Arabs, both regime loyalists and dissenters. Even today, many Sunni Arabs remain unrepentant racist supremacists toward Kurds and wish to reestablish their religious ascendancy over the Shiites.

The Constitution of 2005, ratified by four out of five voters in a UN-validated referendum, restructured British-made Iraq as a voluntary union of its constituent peoples. It proclaims, on paper, a pluralist federation, maps the path toward different and flexible forms of decentralization, and creates multiple incentives for power sharing within a deliberately weak federal government. It remade Iraq as a parliamentary democracy—enabling its Shiite Arab majority to express itself as such, though subject to constitutional restraints, the most important of which lie in the formal strengthening of regions or provinces (governorates) at the expense of what until 2003 had been a series of despotisms in Baghdad.

The Bush administration, despite the mediating role of its ambassador, Zalmay Khalilzad, did not appreciate the Constitution of 2005. Like all U.S. administrations since 1980, it was fixated on having a strong Baghdad "to balance against Iran." This foreign policy preference coincided with the centralist beliefs of the displaced Sunni Arabs and with those of the Sadrists, the followers of Moqtada al-Sadr, and their allies among the Shiites. Since 2005, America's diplomatic muscle has, ironically, been put behind the same constitutional preferences as those who killed American soldiers with frankly reactionary agendas, namely the not-so-ex-Baathists and the Sadrists. The Bush administration, despite nominal good intentions, did not do much to strengthen either liberal or democratic forces in Iraq; it would be tragic if the Obama administration were to repeat the pattern.

The Constitution was made, among the Shiite Arabs, by the leading lights of the Supreme Council for the Islamic Revolution in Iraq, or SCIRI (now renamed the Iraqi Supreme Council of Islam, ISCI), together with the Kurdish leadership. These victims of Saddam agreed that a recentralized Iraq would be a threat to the liberties of Iraq's nationalities, religious communities, and citizens—and to Iraq's neighbors. They determined on a fresh start. They built into the Constitution the recognition of Kurdistan's autonomy, including its right to have its own army, and granted any future regions the right to opt for the same powers as Kurdistan. The Constitution enables any existing provinces—barring Baghdad and Kirkuk—to join with other provinces to form larger regions. Baghdad may become a region in its own right. Provinces not organized in regions have extensive rights of self-government if they choose to exercise them. Special provisions (not yet implemented) enable Kirkuk and other disputed territories to unify with Kurdistan—after the expulsions, gerrymandering, and settler-infusion policies of the Baathists are undone.

The Constitution, in short, permits either a symmetrical federation, in which other regions are built with the same powers as Kurdistan, or an asymmetrical federation, in which the existing provinces of Arab-majority Iraq, by comparison with the KRG, choose to grant greater authority to the Baghdad government.

The Constitution remains a coherent vision of how to remake Iraq as a feasible democracy. It is also Iraq's fundamental law, even if it is often disrespected. The Constitution is, however, in danger—a danger that may be aggravated by misreading Iraq's 2009 provincial elections. No elections were held in Kurdistan and Kirkuk—approximately a fifth of the country. A common and facile evaluation claims that the elections in the fourteen Arab-majority provinces were won by centralists. It is true that ISCI, the champion of a Shiite-dominated southern super-region, was defeated—for now. It lost ground, however, mostly because of its poor performance in the provincial governments and because it was tarred as the Persian party. The fragmented Sunni and Shiite centralists who made advances have utterly rival visions of who should hold power in Baghdad. Moreover, each provincial government will want to exercise its powers as violence subsides and as the incompetence of Baghdad's administration becomes more evident. (The federal oil ministry, for example, has failed to spend more than a fraction of its investment budget for three years in a row.)

In no province did any Arab party or list win 50 percent of the vote, and in only one did any list come close. This voting pattern will therefore lead to multiparty coalition governments in every Arab-majority province. Power sharing, both within provinces and within the federal government, is the unavoidable consequence of proportional representation and of political fragmentation among Arab Iraqis. It makes federalism viable and necessary; it is what Iraq needs, not a strongman backed by Washington.

The Obama administration must not follow the Bush administration, the Baker-Hamilton Report, the Brookings Institution, and other Washington think tanks in the misguided project of aiding the recentralization of Iraq. Some claim that recentralization is the settled will of Arab Iraqis. That is misleading. What Arabs currently reject is aggregating provinces into regions, like Kurdistan. They do not reject empowering their own provinces. And even if they were all full-blooded centralists, they cannot constitutionally weaken Kurdistan's powers. It has an entrenched veto over amendments that might do so. Breaking the Constitution would send Kurdistan toward secession.

It will be far better for the Obama administration to organize an early exit before any Baghdad-based government becomes too strong. In the interim, it should render military and policing assistance to the provinces and to the Kurdistan region—which would be lawful—rather than to federal forces. The reason is simple: to consolidate a balance of power. The weaker a Baghdad government is, the more it must bargain with and accommodate Kurds, Sunni Arabs, and other minorities, and the more it must avoid naked partisanship on behalf of any community. The weaker it is, the greater the prospects for province-based federalism to strengthen itself in Arab Iraq.

This is not the current U.S. wisdom. Obama and Secretary of State Clinton are being encouraged to support the incumbent prime minister, Nuri al-Maliki, on the grounds that he is a secular centralist, as well as the victor of the provincial elections. In fact, he is a deeply insecure but sectarian Shia, and in no Shiite-majority province (ten of Iraq's eighteen) did his list win as much as 40 percent of the vote. He has dictatorial inclinations, but faces a federal Parliament in the year ahead in which numerous parties have incentives to remove him from power before he becomes a viable dictator, or before his party becomes Patronage Central.

Maliki has acted unconstitutionally, and with deliberate provocation, in blocking the implementation of constitutional mandates on natural resources and resolution of the problem of Kirkuk and the disputed territories, and in trying to raise his own unauthorized militia among former Baathists and former Kurdish *jash* (levies from Kurdish tribes who cooperated with Saddam). He has nearly provoked fighting between the federal army and Kurdistan's army in Khanaqin and seemed to want to do the same in Kirkuk. Maliki's goals are transparent: he wants to create a strong central government, led by him.

For the United States to invest wholly in Maliki would be as foolhardy as investing with Bernard Madoff after the warning signals were evident. Obama should support Iraq's Constitution and its federal, multiparty coalition government, but not over-invest in a particular and uncertain person, especially one showing signs of dictatorial enthusiasm. His administration should encourage power sharing, not power centralization, within the workings of the federal executive: Maliki heads a multiparty parliamentary coalition; he is not an executive president. Iraq has sufficient order to make federalism work. It does not need another dictatorship, Sunni or Shiite.

Once the Obama administration questions the idée fixe that Iraq must be recentralized, as Biden did in his capacity as chair of the Senate Foreign Relations Committee, it will realize that it is much wiser to adopt a pro-Constitution policy, not just because it is legally and democratically better, but because it will enable a more judicious and just U.S. exit.

Defusing Tensions Within

There is no point in building up a strong Baghdad military if that leads to a renewed war with Kurdistan. It would repeat the pattern of Iraqi history since 1920. Each successive Iraqi regime that has sought to consolidate its power has broken its previous commitments to Kurdistan's autonomy and sought to conquer it. Ensuing Arab-Kurdish wars have then encouraged interventions by the neighboring powers. It is time to end this cycle.

Washington must therefore seek to resolve major Kurdish-Arab tensions before it leaves. That way Iraq's internal territorial boundaries will be clarified, and the prospects of subsequent Turkish and Iranian interventions reduced. The means are clear—supporting the implementation of the Constitution's Article 140, which, executed fairly, will facilitate Kirkuk's and other disputed territories' unifying with the KRG, in line with local majority opinion. As a quid pro quo, Washington should promote power-sharing provisions in the KRG's Constitution for the Turkomen, Arabs, and Christians of Kirkuk city and offer to monitor minority rights protections that the Kurds have already promoted in good faith. Such a policy would also require supporting the formal transfer into the KRG of the Kurdish majority districts and sub-districts currently below its southern boundary. Such a policy is just: Saddam drew the existing borders, not elected Kurds or Arabs. It is required: the Kurdistan region's boundary does not coincide with existing provincial boundaries, creating an administrative mess. The policy is constitutional. And it is democratic at the relevant level—the local one: Kurdistan's lists appear to have triumphed throughout nearly all the disputed territories in the recent provincial elections. The policy will be stabilizing—provided the Turkomen are appropriately accommodated. A satisfied Kurdistan will be a champion of a federal Iraq. By contrast, a U.S. withdrawal before the just implementation of Article 140 will lead to war between factions in Baghdad and Kurdistan.

Kurdistan rejoined Iraq through the 2005 Constitution. It fears key provisions will not be implemented, and that Maliki and other Arab leaders are determined to build patronage and win votes by making Kurds the scapegoats for the Arabs' civil war and America's occupation. Kurds have observed a succession of U.S. ambassadors who have failed meaningfully to support Iraq's 2005 Constitution. They expect further pressure from the Obama administration to appease Sunni Arab sentiments. But they have gone as far as they can to make Iraq work. The Kurdish leadership will go no further unless the status of Kirkuk and the disputed territories is resolved. They can be squeezed no more without losing the support of their public.

The naïve in Washington are celebrating the provincial electoral successes in Mosul and Basra of those who nominally support a strong centralized Iraq. But, these currently locally successful factions, at polar ends of urban Arab Iraq, do not have much in common—other than a determination for their respective co-religionists to dominate from Baghdad. The not-so-ex-Baathists are not going to be stable coalition partners with Maliki's faction within Dawa, or with the Sadrists. What they promise is little more than competition over who will organize the first coup. They are jointly opposed to greater regionalization—as advocated by ISCI and the Kurds—but they cannot easily govern together, and they cannot change the Constitution radically without Kurdistan's consent. Reversing Bush's mistakes does not require the United States to embrace Baathist and Sadrist agendas.

After the United States exits, an Arab civil war may reignite, along with Kurdish-Arab conflict. The Baathists' and jihadists' response to the U.S. intervention was to promote deliberate societal collapse. They fomented a sectarian Arab civil war rather than accept a Shia-led democratic Iraq. Americans and Kurds did not loot Arab cities, organize suicide bombings against Shiite pilgrims, or provoke sectarian expulsions. It was militants from among Sunni Arabs, Baathists, and Islamists—encouraged by U.S. Secretary of Defense Donald Rumsfeld's blindly repressive military strategy—who precipitated the bloodletting. The resulting violence has only just calmed down. It could be rekindled. The calmer environment exists because the jihadists and Baathists lost. Sunni Arab leaders realized that they could not win the restoration they sought, no matter how extreme their tactics. Some decided it was better to make an alliance with the United States, through the Awakening Councils/Sons of Iraq, rather than go down to comprehensive defeat. General David Petraeus, commander of U.S. forces in Iraq, was able to take advantage of this opportunity. The surge stopped the Sunni Arabs from being utterly "cleansed" from Baghdad.

A key question for the Obama administration is how to facilitate the reincorporation of Sunni Arabs into the new Iraq, but without doing so at the expense of either our Kurdish allies or the Shiites in federal and provincial governments. The answer lies only in the Constitution: encouraging Sunni Arabs to take control of the provinces in which they are now formal electoral majorities and of their own security, through the development of provincial policing. That is the right message to take from recent elections. This policy need not be provocative so long as the Sunni Arabs' boundary disputes with Kurdistan are resolved. If they are, then Sunni Arabs will be free to govern themselves without a significant Kurdish presence in their provinces. The answer to Sunni Arab disaffection does not lie in expanding federal military forces and trying to integrate large numbers of former insurgents—therein lies a recipe for a coup.

Avoiding a Reckless Exit

A responsible exit requires concentrated diplomacy to deter malign interventions. The U.S. withdrawal from Iraq will reduce Iran's interests in destabilizing the new Iraq, provided the United States does not engage in a new bout of hubris and directly aim at regime change in Tehran (what former UN ambassador John Bolton and the last stranded platoons of the Bush administration want). Indeed, pursuing détente with Iran and a new policy with Turkey are both independently appropriate. They will be easier and more cost effective than the false project of rebuilding a strong Baghdad government.

If U.S. policy is rethought in favor of détente with Iran, then balancing Baghdad against Tehran can be abandoned as an overriding U.S. goal. In April 2003, Iran was ready to entertain a grand bargain with the United States over Iraq, in return for being removed from the so-called axis of evil. Skeptics will find the details in Trita Parsi's *Treacherous Alliance: The Secret Dealings of Israel, Iran, and the United States* (especially Appendices A–C). The offer was rejected by the Bush administration, then at the height of its arrogance. Tehran's fear that its regime would be next on Washington's kill list led it to play havoc with the U.S. occupation of Iraq, to restart its nuclear program, and to cause other major difficulties for the United States in the Middle East.

Unwinding Bush's errors with Iran is still feasible. Détente offers the only plausible way simultaneously to facilitate nuclear disarmament in the region, to control the negative consequences of an American withdrawal from Iraq, and to aid Iran's reformers without interfering in Tehran's domestic politics. Nothing here is easy, but it can be done.

The reengineering of U.S. policy toward Turkey is also necessary if we are to leave Iraq responsibly. Turkey fears an independent Kurdistan. But a secure KRG within a federal Iraq will not be an independent Kurdistan; rather, it will be a satisfied, prosperous secular region, a buffer between Turkey and hard-line Islamists. Turkey wants the KRG's cooperation with respect to the Kurdistan Workers' Party (PKK) and its adjunct Party for a Free Life in Kurdistan (PJAK). It will get this, but only if it pays the appropriate price: fully recognizing the KRG and Iraq's Constitution, and avoiding provocations in Kirkuk.

In the past, U.S. administrations have supported Turkey's military—as self-defined guardians of the Enlightenment in former

Ottoman lands. Turkish generals fear democracy because it means the election of soft Islamists and Kurds. Realists in the Obama administration will prefer Turkish generals. They will be at odds with those who want to support Turkey's democratic promise and who want to encourage its journey into Europe. It is the largest sovereign Muslim majority state in the Middle East that allows genuine democratic electoral competition, although it is deeply flawed in its respect for Kurdish and Alawi freedom and in the constraints it puts on public debate. It would be utterly perverse for Obama to abandon a liberalizing and pro-democratic orientation toward Turkey. U.S. policy should be firm—seeking Turkey's respect for the sovereignty of Iraq and of its Constitution, which recognizes the KRG. It should also be wise—supporting Turkey's deepening democratization at the expense of its military and, if necessary, recognizing Turkey's existing border through a treaty. If the Obama administration mismanages its exit from Iraq, it could be faced with new military dictators in both Ankara and Baghdad. Sacrificing Iraq's Kurds is not the way to eliminate that scenario.

The federal government remains, for now, in the hands of a multiparty coalition, in which the Kurds, ISCI, and others want to remove Maliki from the premiership if they can. The Kurds, with good reason, fear he wishes to establish a dictatorship and to block their gains in order to build clients among traditional Arab nationalists. ISCI wants to recover lost ground and to prevent Dawa from permanently gaining at its expense. The Kurds and ISCI have had a small Sunni partner, in the Iraqi Islamic Party, that did better than expected in the provincial elections, but its trajectory is uncertain.

Maliki presents himself as a source of stability, above faction. He is anything but. He stays in power through buying off a combustible combination of Baathists, Sunni tribal leaders, and Sadrists, and by retaining U.S. backing. He has benefited from an exhausted Arab public's urgent thirst for order, but in no province commands a majority, and his next steps promise disorder.

Before the next federal elections, Maliki will want American support to prevent his removal by the Kurds and ISCI (who still have far larger numbers in the Baghdad federal legislature than in the provinces). The Sunni Arabs will want the Americans to integrate the entirety of the Awakening Councils into the federal forces, which would represent the restoration of Sunni predominance within the army. That would mean a future of attempted coups. The Sadrists, recovering from recent wounds, want a centralized Iraq, at the expense of the Kurds (loud voice), and at the expense of the Sunni Arabs (quiet voice). The United States is therefore set to be wooed by the Arab factions most hostile to the new Constitution, those most likely to attempt coups, and those most likely to re-start civil wars.

The Obama administration should realize that the Kurdish parties, ISCI, the Iraqi Islamic Party, and some sections of Dawa are those most likely to consolidate the new Iraq as a pluralist federation. It should use its soft power to facilitate them. The Bush administration blocked Kurdistan's lawful use of Article 112 to develop its natural resources. Ambassador Ryan Crocker was the latest in a series of U.S. emissaries to deter major U.S. oil and gas companies from investing in Kurdistan. This policy was not only against Iraq's Constitution, it also prevented Kurdistan from aiding Iraq's economic recovery. The Bush administration then hypocritically stood aside and insisted that the implementation of Article 140 on boundaries was a purely internal matter. In so doing, it blocked the democratic resolution of territorial boundaries, which is essential if Iraq is to be stable after America's departure. Switching both policies around would be constitutionally correct and would pay political dividends. The United States should also offer its good offices to aid the committees currently trying to resolve disputes between Baghdad and the KRG—on boundaries, natural resources, budgetary allocations, and security. And it should encourage the provincialization of security, to stabilize Sunni Arab majority provinces. But settling the internal boundaries is crucial; without that, no responsible exit is possible.

If the Obama administration does none of these things, it will not be able to wash its hands of the blood that will flow as a result of a reckless exit. An exit designed by those who call themselves realists would return to power—not only in Baghdad, but also in Ankara and Tehran—those who most oppose everything that Obama stands for—liberal, democratic, tolerant, and multiracial pluralism.

11

It Isn't Over

GEORGE PACKER

MOST Americans think the war in Iraq is over, or should be over, or will be over very soon. Whether we won or lost is less certain and has already become the subject of a debate that will grow more intense over the next few years. One side of this debate is setting up the new president to bear the full blame just in case things should unravel under his administration—a preemptive "Who lost Iraq?" war. According to Charles Krauthammer, writing in the *Washington Post* just before the inauguration, President Barack Obama "will be loath to jeopardize the remarkable turnaround in American fortunes in Iraq. Obama opposed the war. But the war is all but over. What remains is an Iraq turned from aggressive, hostile power in the heart of the Middle East to an emerging democracy openly allied with the United States. No president would want to be responsible for undoing that success." In other words, Iraq is looking so good that Obama can only screw it up. In April 2003, just before the fall of Baghdad, Thomas Friedman wrote a *New York Times* column titled "Hold Your

Applause." A few weeks later, at an NBA basketball game, Friedman ran into Krauthammer, who smirked, "Still holding your applause?" Six years later, it's apparently safe to applaud, again—which only proves that the partisan wishful thinking that did so much harm before the invasion and during the early years of the war has re-emerged undaunted, just in time to fix Barack Obama in its sights.

On the other side, Obama's campaign pledge to have combat troops out in 2010 has become an article of faith that can be converted into a stick. "We have no reason to think Obama's backed off his campaign promises on a timeline to end the war," Eli Pariser of Moveon.org told the *Times* soon after the inauguration. Medea Benjamin of Code Pink wrote in *USA Today*, "The American people want our troops out. The best reflection of this is that they elected Barack Obama to lead us out of Iraq. . . . The presence of U.S. troops ensures ongoing violence by attracting armed opposition and postpones the day of reckoning among Iraqi factions."

Two things should be clear by now. The first is that American troops, while never popular among Iraqis, have lately been the only force that could reduce violence enough to give Iraqi factions a chance to meet their day of political reckoning. The winter provincial elections, which took place almost without violence, were the first in which Iraqis were able to vote for normal things—services, security, clean government—instead of for identity-group power in a zero-sum death struggle. The second is that no one can be sure whether or not Iraq will plunge back into apocalyptic levels of violence, and that, after so many years of killing in Iraq and foolishness in Washington, nothing that can be called victory is possible. To speak of winning is obscene—which is perhaps one reason why General David Petraeus and most other rational officers refuse to use the word. The views of ideologues on both sides have never had anything to do with the realities in Iraq. There's no reason why that should change under a new administration, as America finally begins to withdraw.

Most Americans have no political stake in Iraq's success or fail-ure. They are simply tired of the war. To hear about American sol-diers and Marines still dying in Iraq is almost an embarrassment to fellow citizens back home, who have long since stopped think-ing about it. A Marine Corps major recently sent me eight long let-ters he had written home from Ramadi, where he was stationed in ·2005. "I thought that you might find them interesting if only as pri-mary source testimonial from a bleary part of the front," he wrote. "Enjoy if that is possible and thank you for paying attention. Very few have." Of course, this is the fate of soldiers who come home from every war, even wars that are short and end in a clear victory: no one at home really wants to hear about it. After finishing his World War I novel *Three Soldiers*, a couple of years after the armistice, John Dos Passos learned that publishers were already wary of war fiction, and he had a very hard time finding one who would publish his. Public indifference, tinged with shame, is much greater in the case of a long, ambiguous, unnecessary war like Iraq. Are we still over there? Why can't we just leave and let them sort it out? After six years of war, this is the overwhelming and entirely understandable feeling among Americans.

We will leave, one way or another. Barack Obama has made this clear: he wants to turn the country's attention and effort away from Iraq and toward Afghanistan. And the government of Iraq has also expressed its view—in the form of a status of forces agreement that was painfully negotiated in the last days of the Bush administration—that it wants American troops out of Iraq by the end of 2011. It's possible that, when the time comes, another Iraqi government will want to renegotiate the agreement and keep some residual American force around longer. With Obama's announcement that all combat units will be withdrawn by August 2010, the direction of America in Iraq is clear: we are heading for the exits.

A Paced Withdrawal

How we leave still matters very much, because the war is neither Charles Krauthammer's all-but-certain victory nor Medea Benjamin's unmitigated catastrophe. The outcome still hangs in the balance, and the outcome still matters to us. Most of what happens in Iraq is now out of our control—that's been true to some degree all along—but we still hold the default position of being able to prevent the worst without guaranteeing the good. For this reason, what one should hope from the president is that he will not leave Iraq with the same indifference to facts and nuances that characterized his predecessor's invading it. He should be as pragmatic about the war as his admirers say he is about everything else. Though there will be many other things, Afghanistan among them, that will demand his powers of focus, Obama should not stop paying attention to Iraq. The last thing he should seek there is vindication.

In a discussion on washingtonpost.com in early 2009, military analyst Stephen Biddle argued that U.S. forces are now carrying out the function of peacekeeping in Iraq, not counterinsurgency or counterterrorism, and he compared this role to the one we played in the Balkans in the 1990s:

> We began with a large peacekeeping force, but within four years of the ceasefires in Bosnia and Kosovo those peacekeeping forces had been reduced by about half without reigniting the warfare. And today our forces in both countries are just a fraction of what they once were. If we apply that logic to Iraq, it doesn't call for a "permanent surge"—but it does suggest that a continued sizeable presence for several more years could help stabilize a situation that, by analogy to other comparable cases elsewhere, one might worry could be prone to renewed violence otherwise. Elsewhere I've argued that a good drawdown timeline (again by analogy to the Balkans) might be a 50 percent cut by 2011; obviously there are now a number of constraints—e.g. the status of forces

agreement—that complicate the question of how long we should stay with how many forces. Iraq is a sovereign nation—if they ask us to leave we should and must. But if we have the flexibility to do it, my own view is that stability would be served by a slower drawdown rather than a faster one.

Iraq will be lucky if it becomes as stable as Bosnia or Kosovo. And the fact that America was invader, occupier, and counterinsurgent before it became peacekeeper further complicates the analogy. But it's a useful reminder of the critical role we now play, the delicacy of the current truce, and the folly of leaving strictly on our terms rather than Iraq's. We should withdraw as slowly as domestic political pressure, military requirements elsewhere, and Iraqi opinion allow. Local realities, and the fingertip feel that comes with hard experience, will count for more than policies formed on the basis of a new strategic vision. A brewing tribal feud in Anbar could be more important than an intergovernmental policy review. It will be particularly important for Obama to be willing to hear from his commanders in Iraq bad news that could intrude on his best-laid plans—to learn that Diyala or Mosul remains too volatile for a scheduled withdrawal, for example, but will take another six months or year, with American combat units still close to Iraqi population centers.

Those units, stationed in patrol bases and assigned the mission of securing civilians, were the necessary, though not sufficient, condition for most of Iraq to become stable over the past two years. According to Thomas Ricks's *The Gamble*, Petraeus and his staff went into Baghdad in early 2007 with grim expectations for the success of the surge. They wanted above all to buy themselves time; what followed was unpredictable in advance but understandable and to an extent controllable as it unfolded. The same will be true of this next stage of the war, which will see the end of large-scale American military involvement in Iraq. We don't know what will follow an

American departure from Iraqi cities (it didn't go very well when we tried in the past), but we should buy ourselves as much understanding and control as possible.

During the campaign, Obama was sometimes asked about the potential for genocide in the wake of American departure. Having made genocide in Darfur and even Congo a moral issue, he could hardly dismiss its prospect in Iraq, and so Obama replied that he would order American forces to intervene and stop it if genocide broke out. Since 2007, a number of things have happened to make such a catastrophe less likely: the Iraqi army has become a more unifying and professional national force; sectarian cleansing during the civil war has already separated most Sunni and Shia in fortified enclaves; and traditional Sunni power brokers have begun to accept that there's no going back to the status quo ante. Violence is more likely to occur between Arabs and Kurds and among Shia and Sunni factions, which for various reasons would be unlikely to lead to killings on a genocidal scale.

But if the worst happens, an American return to the cities after withdrawals begin would be very difficult in both political and practical terms. Once our forces leave, first to large bases and then across the border, it would be almost impossible for them to go back in, because the American people would oppose the huge risks that a renewed intervention would place on troops at such a late stage of the war. And large-scale massacres could not be stopped by forces already well outside the ethnic and sectarian enclaves where the killings might take place. To be in a position to intervene, we would have to still be patched onto the shredded fabric of Iraqi society, with all the early-warning intelligence and tactical advantages that come with it. We wouldn't be able to stop genocide from a forward operating base in the desert or the highway to Kuwait. Obama's campaign answer always had the feel of a politician with strong moral views about genocide and no appetite to get more deeply involved in Iraq. The best way to prevent Iraq from returning to chaos is to leave slowly.

How We Leave

The strategic reasons for keeping Iraq stable and continuing to strengthen its national government seem clear enough. Here are half a dozen: Al Qaeda, oil, regional security, Iranian influence, humanitarian concern, and America's reputation in the Arab-Muslim world. The moral responsibility we bear for Iraq's destruction and our strategic interest in putting it back together point in the same direction. Even as we wind down our military presence, we should remain involved politically and diplomatically, both in Baghdad and through such instruments as the provincial reconstruction teams that are helping to rebuild governments and economies around the country. Having wasted colossal amounts of money in Iraq, the United States shouldn't try to balance the books by shortchanging important development efforts that, now that there's a reasonable level of security, stand a chance of showing some success. Finally, even after the last combat brigades are withdrawn in 2010, the tens of thousands of residual American forces will not be based in a secure and peaceful country: as Thomas Ricks has written, in Iraq there is no such thing as a non-combat unit, and the remaining troops will inevitably be involved in violent missions that result in American casualties. The president should be candid with the public about this prospect and head off the demand for every last soldier and Marine to be withdrawn.

Another way to preserve our interests and discharge our responsibilities is by making a much greater effort than the previous administration to solve the huge problem of displaced Iraqis—numbering in the millions—both inside Iraq and in neighboring countries. One aspect of a solution is for the United States to be as generous to Iraqi refugees and asylum seekers trying to come here as Sweden has been, or as the United States was at the end of the Vietnam War. (After abandoning thousands of Vietnamese allies in the chaotic evacuation, the Ford administration reversed course and rewrote or ignored immigration rules, resettling 130,000 Vietnamese in the United States by the end of 1975.) The bureaucratic obstacles with which the Bush administration prevented more than a trickle of Iraqis from entering the country are one of the lasting shames of the war. The fact that this stinginess extended to Iraqis who risked their lives by working with American troops and officials in Iraq makes the disgrace complete.

Our true Iraqi allies—not the politicians living in the safety of the Green Zone, but the interpreters, drivers, contractors, and office workers who make the dangerous commute from home to work and back every day—number in the tens of thousands. Thus far, those who have gained entry to the United States number in the hundreds. Recently, bipartisan pressure from Congress, as well as statements by Ryan Crocker, the most recent American ambassador in Baghdad, have pushed the doors open a little wider. Iraqis no longer have to become refugees outside their country before they can apply for re-settlement to the United States; processing has begun at the American embassy in Baghdad. But the obstacles remain daunting.

Those Iraqis who worked for Americans will probably never be able to live without fear in their own country; whatever the general security, if their jobs become known they will be marked for death and helpless to defend themselves. And if Iraq ever does become a place where they can live openly and freely, it will surely need their professional skills and liberal views. When the British withdrew from downtown Basra to the air base outside the city, they failed to make arrangements to protect their Iraqi employees, and almost immediately local militias began a killing spree. (This tragedy and the outrage it provoked helped push the government of Prime Minister

Gordon Brown to begin an airlift of qualified Iraqis to the United Kingdom.) Multiply the numbers by a factor of fifty or a hundred and you can imagine the scale of the disaster if America begins to close its bases and head for the borders without ensuring the safety of its Iraqi friends.

The simplest way to avert a tragedy and uphold our obligations is to conduct an airlift, like the British and the Danes before them, before large-scale withdrawals begin. This solution is sometimes called "the Guam option," because it would involve flying qualified Iraqis and their families to Guam, where the United States still has large facilities that date back to the Vietnam era, and where they can be processed and vetted in a place where both they and Americans on the mainland remain safe. In 1996, after Saddam Hussein invaded Kurdistan and intervened in a Kurdish civil war, the United States conducted exactly this operation, called "Pacific Safe Haven," managing to fly 7,000 Kurds out of danger and eventually to America. It was a model that could be replicated today, though in admittedly more complicated circumstances. Organizations like the Center for American Progress, the liberal think tank with extensive ties to the Obama administration, and the List Project, a nonprofit organization that seeks to resettle America's Iraqi allies here, have endorsed the Guam option and spelled out in detail what it would require.

There would be a cost, both in dollars and in publicity. It's easy to imagine all the reasons why Obama wouldn't want to initiate such a dramatic and potentially risky operation. It would attract a great deal of attention, even if it were done as quietly as possible, just when Obama is trying to shift the country's focus away from Iraq to the other war. It would stir up outrage among anti-immigrant groups. (It would also win the support of veterans, religious organizations, and Republicans and Democrats of conscience.) The Guam option would make these Iraqis very much the Obama administration's problem.

Even if the new president refuses to pursue such a bold plan, he should understand that the fate of Iraqis who met us halfway in their own country will be the ultimate test for whether America leaves more responsibly than it came. They are a kind of inescapable reminder that, much as we wish our part in the war were over, much as we might wish it had never happened at all, America will have obligations as well as interests in Iraq for a long time to come.

Contributors

Shlomo Avineri, Professor of Political Science at the Hebrew University of Jerusalem, served as director-general of Israel's Ministry of Foreign Affairs in the first government of Prime Minister Yitzhak Rabin. He was a member of the Commission that negotiated the Israeli-Egyptian Cultural and Scientific Agreement. In 1996 he received the Israel Prize, the country's highest civilian decoration. Among his books are *The Social and Political Thought of Karl Marx, Hegel's Theory of the Modern State, Israel and the Palestinians, The Making of Modern Zionism, Moses Hess: Prophet of Communism and Zionism,* and *Communitarianism and Individualism.*

Rajeev Bhargava is director and senior fellow, Centre for the Study of Developing Societies, Delhi. His publications include *Secularism and Its Critics* and *Politics and Ethics of the Indian Constitution* (editor). He wishes to thank Rajeshwari Balasubramian and Shruti

Murlidharan for research assistance and Tani Sandhu for helpful suggestions on this manuscript.

David Bromwich is Sterling Professor of English at Yale University. Among his books are *Politics by Other Means: Higher Education and Group Thinking, Hazlitt: The Mind of a Critic,* and *Disowned by Memory: Wordsworth's Poetry of the 1790s.* He has edited a selection of letters and speeches by Edmund Burke, *On Empire, Liberty, and Reform,* and is completing an intellectual biography of Burke.

Frances FitzGerald is a journalist and author. Her 1972 study of Vietnam, *Fire in the Lake: The Vietnamese and the Americans in Vietnam,* won the Pulitzer Prize, the National Book Award, and the Bancroft Prize. She also wrote *Way Out There in the Blue: Reagan, Star Wars, and the End of the Cold War.*

Stanley Karnow was awarded the Pulitzer Prize in history in 1991 for his book *In Our Image: America's Empire in the Philippines.* His other books include *Mao and China: From Revolution to Revolution* and *Vietnam, a History.* He has reported from Asia for *Time, Life,* the *Washington Post,* and the *London Observer* and is the recipient of six Emmys and two Overseas Press Club awards.

Nicolaus Mills is Professor of American Studies at Sarah Lawrence College. His books include *Like a Holy Crusade: Mississippi 1964, The Triumph of Meanness: America's War Against Its Better Self,* and *Winning the Peace: The Marshall Plan and America's Coming of Age as Superpower.* This essay is from his book in progress, *Run-Up: 9/11 and the Road to Iraq.*

Brendan O'Leary is Lauder Professor of Political Science and Director of the Program in Ethnic Conflict at the University of Pennsylvania.

Among the seventeen books he has written òr edited are *Terror, Insurgency, and the State: Ending Protracted Conflicts, The Future of Kurdistan in Iraq*, and *The Northern Ireland Conflict: Consociational Engagements*. He contributed to the United Nations Human Development Report on Culture and Liberty and since 2003 has been an international constitutional advisor to the Kurdistan Regional Government in Iraq.

George Packer is a staff writer for the *New Yorker*. He was a member of the Peace Corps in Lavie, Togo, from 1982 to 1983. His nonfiction books include *The Village of Waiting, Blood of the Liberals, The Assassins' Gate*, and the forthcoming *Interesting Times: Writings from a Turbulent Decade*. He is the author of the novels *The Half Man* and *Central Square*. He received the Overseas Press Club Award for his reporting from Iraq.

Todd Shepard is an associate professor in the Department of History at Johns Hopkins University. A revised edition of his book *The Invention of Decolonization: The Algerian War and the Remaking of France* has been published in French as *1962: Comment l'indépendance algérienne a transformé la France*.

Fred Smoler teaches history and literature at Sarah Lawrence College. His writing has appeared in *American Heritage Magazine, First of the Month*, the *Observer*, the *Nation*, and the *New York Times*.

Michael Walzer, co-editor of *Dissent*, is Professor Emeritus at the Institute for Advanced Study in Princeton. His books include *Thinking Politically: Essays in Political Theory, Arguing About War, Spheres of Justice*, and *Just and Unjust Wars*.

Stanley Weintraub, Evan Pugh Professor Emeritus of Arts and Humanities at Pennsylvania State University and a Guggenheim Fellow, is the author or editor of more than fifty books of biography and history. Among them are *Aubrey Beardsley: Imp of the Perverse*; *Victoria: An Intimate Biography*; *Disraeli: A Biography*; *MacArthur's War: Korea and the Undoing of an Anmerican Hero*; *Silent Night: The Story of the World War I Christmas Truce*; and *Iron Tears: America's Battle for Freedom, Britain's Quagmire*. As an army officer during the Korean war, he earned a Bronze Star.

Index

Acknowledgments

A COLLABORATIVE project like this book depends on the commitment and work of many people. First of all, it depends on the writers who contributed to it. We are grateful for their willingness to think again about historical cases they had written about before, to write new essays for the magazine, and to revise their essays for the book.

Dissent's office staff were critical to the project. Neil Ellingson, our assistant editor, kept things moving, met all the deadlines, stayed in touch with all the writers, and coordinated our work with the people at Penn Press. David Marcus, our online editor, also read the essays and helped make them better—the Introduction especially. Nick Serpe and Dan Wertz, our 2008-9 interns, did vital fact-checking and joined all the staff discussions about the book and the writers.

Maxine Phillips, *Dissent*'s executive editor and most necessary person, edited all the pieces that appeared in the magazine.

William Finan, our editor at Penn Press, recognized immediately that the articles of *Getting Out* would make a good book and championed the project at the Press, where *Getting Out* was strongly supported by Eric Halpern, Director of Penn Press, and by the members of its editorial board. We are grateful to all of them, and glad to launch this first *Dissent* book under their auspices.